TA
Psychology

Robert Wang

TAROT
Psychology

A Practical Guide
to the
Jungian Tarot

Including a 34 Week
Course of Self-Study

U.S. GAMES SYSTEMS, INC.
Publishers   •   **Stamford, CT 06902 USA**

First published in 1988 in Switzerland by
Urania Verlags AG, CH-8212 Neuhausen

Printed and bound by Arcata Graphics

Library of Congress Catalog Card Number: 91-67095

ISBN 0-88079-366-X

10 9 8 7 6 5 4 3 2 1

Printed in USA

U.S. GAMES SYSTEMS, INC.
179 Ludlow Street
Stamford, CT 06902 USA

Acknowledgments

Sincere thanks are due to fellow-artist Mark Whitehead, whose encouragement, advice, and intelligent criticism over the five-year period of painting the cards has been invaluable.

Thanks are due also to those who have made useful suggestions on the preparation of this manuscript, including: Dr. Gregory Lehne, Department of Psychiatry, Johns Hopkins University, Dr. John Donovan, Department of Philosophy, Georgetown University, Dr. Marilyn Demorest, Department of Psychology, University of Maryland, Sandra Beach, former Director of the Archive for Research in Archival Symbolism of the New York Jung Center, Dr. Edith Wallace, and to other distinguished Jungian scholars whose advice has improved this book.

Special notes of appreciation are due to Karen Montgomery, a talented artist whose criticism of the paintings as they progressed has been of inestimable worth, and to Vincent Messina, whose ideas contributed significantly to the development of a new scheme of interpretation for the cards.

Contents

Introduction

The Jungian Tarot is a visual gateway into the complexities of Jungian psychology. It is a set of precisely interrelated images designed on Jungian principles for a method which Jung described as "active imagination." The goal is the attainment of a state of absolute self-knowledge which he termed "individuation," but which has been more commonly called "enlightenment" by the Western mystery tradition. This means, theoretically, a level of consciousness in which the true nature of life and death is understood.

Carl Jung (1875–1961), a Swiss psychiatrist and colleague of Sigmund Freud, was one of the pioneers of the psychoanalytic movement. He was a creative thinker whose observation of correspondences between world religions, mythologies, and the dreams of his patients led to a unique overview of the human condition. His books are difficult reading, but his basic conclusions are easily outlined:

First, Jung emphasized the reality of the psychic life – a fact which separated him from the empirically-oriented mainstream of academic psychology.

Second, he proposed that all human consciousness is linked together – that the consciousness of each person is like a small pond which trickles into the ocean of a shared "collective unconscious."

The third key principle involves the contents of this collective unconscious – what Jung called *archetypes*. These are "cultural imprints," images and ideas built up by the thoughts of mankind throughout history. Over the centuries there has developed, for example, a generalized concept of "mother." This is a cross-cultural idea seen in mythologies, in fairy tales, and in world religions. The

"Great Mother," or "Mother Earth," appears (especially in dreams) under an incalculable variety of forms. This universal mother can be loving or nurturing, or she can be a sort of Medusa, a hag whose very glance destroys.

Following Jung's suggestion of a relationship between the archetypes and the Tarot, the seventy-eight paintings of *The Jungian Tarot* have been created as "archetypal images." Through them we can begin to tap into the irrational materials of the personal unconscious and then into the collective unconscious realm which, in principle, determines our conscious behavior.

A fourth tenet of Jungian psychology is that everything is based on opposites, male and female. In the Tarot, *The Magician* is the totality of Self, a unity which is the potential for both male and female. All other cards (except *The Fool*) show aspects of one or the other, like separate facets of two crystals which have been broken from a single primordial crystal. Female is shown, among other aspects, as Maiden, as Mother, as Grandmother, as Whore. Man is seen as young boy, as father, as grandfather.

When we meditate on a given Tarot card, we deal with a specific aspect of ourselves. With the *Empress* we address first our own Mother, and then the pure Mother aspect of our own being; the *Emperor* brings us to consider first our own father and then the pure Father in each of us. The ultimate aim is the reintegration of our own opposites, a return to the pristine spiritual state of *The Fool*.

The cards are intended for personal use as well as for interaction between professional psychotherapist and patient. Moreover, *The Jungian Tarot* deck is offered as a rich and varied alternative to earlier diagnostic tools, such as Rorschach, in the belief that the diagnostic validity of such currently popular projective measures depends more upon the interpretive competence of the psychologist than upon the devices themselves.

Some may disagree and may, responding to our "Age of Science's" rather negative social-toning of the Tarot cards as "occult," casually dismiss even the possibility that these pictures could have serious clinical and self-analytical worth.

However, it should be understand that until our own century, when a psychological vocabulary was developed for the first time, a wide range of human emotions, ideas, states of consciousness, and even interpersonal relationships, were *symbolized* by planets, by animals, and even by graphic forms such as crosses, circles, and squares. A great deal of what has come to be known as "occult" was the attempt of our forbears to describe the complexities of consciousness. Such descriptions were invariably related to religious movements.

Of course, the *Jungian Tarot* is not intended to foster belief in any mythological, occult, or religious system. To use these cards effectively one need not espouse any program of ideas — not even the essential Jungian postulate of archetypes of the collective unconscious. The core method here is very pragmatic. One need only approach these cards with a "willing suspension of disbelief," and then draw personal conclusions about the results of their use under given circumstances.

Those who are analytically-inclined, and who are open to the premise that the Tarot offers a more detailed and precise configuration of archetypal interactions than any other symbolic pantheon, will be rewarded by applying Tarot patterns to mythology and to fairy tales such as those collected by the brothers Grimm in the mid-nineteenth century.

The wicked witch may, for example, be considered to be the destructive aspect of the Mother shown as *The Moon*; the Wise Old Man, the Grandfather as Teacher, may be viewed as an aspect of Spirit which is *The Hermit*; and the Handsome Prince, the Experience-Gathering Son may be

13

called *The Magician* and *The Lover.*

The recurrence of such figures in fairy tales, and the extent to which their familial interactions are consistent with those of the Tarot figures, leads one to the inescapable conclusion that Tarot cards and fairy tales refer to identical activities of the archetypes of the collective unconscious. This relationship between the personalities found in Tarot and in folk legend is considered in some detail in another companion book to the cards, *The Jungian Tarot: An Iconological Study in Cross-Cultural Archetypal Imagery.* (Robert Wang, Urania, 1988)

In more practical terms, meditation on the the 22 Tarot Keys, showing various aspects of male and female, leads to an *objective* overview of the human condition. The Court cards (Kings, Queens, Princes, and Princesses) represent types of personalities. The behavior and activities of these personalities is shown by the The Minor Cards (Ace-Ten) what Jung called "Archetypes of Transformation," meaning potential or actual situations and events. Together the Court and Minor Cards promote understanding of the ways in which we deal *subjectively* with different people and life experiences.

Aspects of Self are also symbolized by a *Mandala* at the base of each Tarot Key. The Mandala, a "magic circle" used as an aid to contemplation in the East, is a more graphic way of suggesting the energies of the many archetypes connected to each card.

Attribution of Meanings to the Cards

The Jungian Tarot is a very flexible device which can be used with any system. There are no captions on the cards, either to distract in meditation, or to impose a specific sequential order. Readers are free to apply whatever interpretive programs they may consider appropriate.

However, those who choose to accept the so-called

"traditional" interpretations should be aware that these ideas are not only of recent origin, but are frequently quite arbitrary. Nineteenth century esoteric fraternities did develop creative, and still acceptable, attributions for the Major Arcana, but their often eccentric patterns of interpretation for the Minor Cards must be reconsidered.

In an attempt to make Tarot studies more consistent with other aspects of Western mystery tradition, this book proposes a complete revision of attributions to the Court and Minor cards. Meanings are based on an outline so simple that anyone who has studied astrology will know the value of a card immediately. The way by which such interpretations have been derived is explained in the section *Rationale for the Assignment of Attributions*.

A scheme based upon astrology, and upon Hermetic-Qabalistic philosophy, offers a very workable and efficient set of values for the cards. Such meanings have been developed over at least three thousand years. Tarot, obviously, has no such ancient tradition of interpretation.

Practical Work with the Jungian Tarot Cards

Page 121 begins an outline of a self-study course applying Jungian methods of active imagination, which requires a significant commitment of time and effort. But results appear faster, and are more profound, than with most other Western systems of meditation, because everything relates to the solving of real-life problems. There is far less possibility of "escapism" in this method than there is in other systems claiming to encourage direct encounter with one's own inner self.

Readers are encouraged to quickly peruse the following descriptive text on the 78 cards, and to then turn to the section describing a 34 week program of self-examination with the cards.

THE FOOL

Spirit: The Source

A young man, carrying the spark of life symbolized by a flaming rose, is about to step off into a starry sky. This act will create a universe to eventually be destroyed by the panther at his right. At his left is the Orphic Egg in which the Cosmos is nurtured. The Crown above refers to that which is the unified source of All, that which directs and controls the framework of consciousness at all levels.

An encounter with this card is unlike that of any other. Symbolically, *The Fool* is the youthful aspect of Spirit which embodies all potential, and from which all other cards of the Tarot derive; so conversation with this figure tends to be a great deal more philosophical than with the rest of the Keys.

In practice, *The Fool* may change shape often, and may appear in extraordinary ways – sometimes conveying a great sense of peace, and at other times creating fear that is beyond description (the exercise of self-discovery is not for the faint-hearted). We may converse with a child, a youth, an old man, a dragon, a crocodile, or with some other animal. *The Fool* may appear as a ball of light or as a thunderstorm. What we deal with here is the nature of the creative act within ourselves. This card represents the totality of Self, the Godhead of individual consciousness. In conversation with *The Fool* we address the totality of our own capacities. And we may ask some extremely difficult questions: Who am I? Where do I come from? Where do I go?

The deeper our meditation with this card, the closer we come to the very ideological source of the unconscious, the more profound, and usually the more irrational, the answers we "receive" become. Commonly, many people feel that encounter with this figure produces either no results, or results which are more than absurd. But what is represented is far beyond thought, and the effects of addressing its energies may be most disquieting to a mind which sees reality only in terms of the waking consciousness. It is, thus, advisable that meditation with *The Fool* be postponed until experience has been gained with other cards.

There is nothing to fear. But advanced discrimination skills are required to make sense of the experiences which are likely to result from interaction with this archetypal figure.

THE MAGICIAN

The Son

The Magician is the celestial alchemist, the ultimate director of the quest for Self. He is the author of Sun and Moon. He is at once the potential for all opposites and the means for their reconciliation. As Mercurius he is the "Messenger of the Gods."

The primary archetype associated with this card (each card actually embodies myriad archetypes, a few of which are most significant) is *Animus*, a latin word meaning *soul* chosen by Jung to mean the female *contrasexual component*. Jung stated that deep inside of every woman there is a male figure, *Animus*, and that every man has within himself a female figure, *Anima* (latin: spirit). These are real personalities which inhabit the unconscious, and with which we interact especially in dreams. Anima and Animus are our inner antagonists; they are guides into the caverns of our own minds.

When a man talks about Animus he does so as an outsider. But to a woman, this inner figure is very real. He is the epitome of male. He is father, brother, husband, son. He is one whose characteristics reflect the traditional male role throughout history, including demand of respect, and a tendency to be quite argumentative.

In this, the assignment of this archetype to Magician/Mercury is completely appropriate. Mercury was the creator of language, and Animus loves to expound on things, can be very wordy, and does not like to admit that he is ever wrong. Moreover, he may change his mind as quickly as he may change the form in which he appears.

For a woman *The Magician* is the most important card in the deck. For a man the same may be said of *The High Priestess*. These are the essential cards of male and of female from which all other archetypal figures derive. A woman's whole quest for self-discovery is encapsulated in her relationship to *The Magician*, Animus.

Jung states that this very complex archetype can appear not just as a single figure, but can be a group of some sort, such as a panel of judges! *Mercurius* is also the archetype of the Trickster. *The Magician* makes things up as he goes along, and will lie if it amuses him to do so. Considerable discrimination is required here, and many of the points which can be made about *The Fool* can also be made about this card.

THE HIGH PRIESTESS

The Daughter

Anima is the inner self of a man. She is eternal woman who, as *The High Priestess*, holds a book symbolizing the ultimate secrets of the unconscious — most frequently represented by *water*. As the Moon, she creates the universal tides of consciousness.

Everyone has an inner personality (Anima or Animus), and an outer personality, the *Persona* or mask — that which we show to the public. In this card the mask has been pulled aside to reveal the true face of Anima whereas in the card specific to Persona, *The World*, the inner face is completely hidden.

It is a general principle that inner and outer personalities are complementary: a very methodical and scientific Persona usually suggests an emotional and irrational inner being.

As was stated of Animus, the encounter of Anima, especially in dreams, is a very real experience. Her activity as antagonist, always at work in a man, brings softness, emotionality, love of beautiful things and of home, etc., the many qualities which western society has generally attributed to female. Here one may rightly assume that as society's perception of male and female evolves, so will the individual's interaction with Anima or with Animus.

In meditation, Christians may experience Anima as the Virgin Mary, although her characteristics are more accurately described through the polarities of the ancient gods. She is all phases of woman, the mother Hera, the virgin Diana, the hag Hecate. She can be loving and supportive, friendly and charming, or she can be deceptive, cruel, and very arbitrary.

It is essential to understand that every archetype has two aspects — positive and negative, both of which must be encountered in the quest for self-knowledge. Tarot interpretation has generally focused on the positive aspects of the Major Arcana. But the creative *Fool* also destroys; the protectively controlling *Magician* can lie and cheat; the coldly beautiful virgin *High Priestess* can be ugly and coarse.

However she may appear when, through active imagination, this archetype is invoked and a conversation begun, the effect is inevitably powerful. It may also be unpredictable as contents of the unconscious are brought closer to the surface.

THE EMPRESS

The Mother

The Empress is seated on a throne amidst a profusion of foliage. Her expression is serene and benevolent, for her role is that of fruitful and kindly mother. She holds a golden cup symbolizing the *yoni*, the female generative organ.

But we understand that, in the most abstract sense, she is, herself, the Cup.

Behind the Empress is a lake symbolizing the unconscious, and referring to her "Virgin" phase as the *High Priestess*. But in these waters swims a deadly serpent, meaning that destructive aspect of the mother whom we shall meet as the archetypal figure of Hecate in *The Moon*. Other aspects of the mother are shown emerging from the leaves at her feet: the Dove is that of Venus, who is the Goddess of Love; the cave at bottom left is to suggest that as Mother Earth, she is also the ruler of the Underworld, what Jung refers to as the "Chthonic" realm.

The Mother Archetype is very pivotal to the process of self-understanding, especially for a man. "Mother" is an extension of the qualities of Anima; she is the nurturing aspect of Anima which assumes special importance in Jungian psychology.

Jung devoted considerable attention to the interactions between archetypal Mother and archetypal Son — a relationship which must be understood at many levels. Symbolically, there is nothing in manifestation but Male and Female which through their interaction produce the Son (and, thus, they become Father and Mother), who is the perfect balance of their opposites, and who is the "Perfected Self."

Certainly, the metaphysical philosophy surrounding this card is complex. But encounter with the Mother archetype is inevitably direct and is often very emotional, especially as we initially consider our relationship with our own mother. It is only by unearthing those unconscious materials relating to interaction with our mother (both good and bad), and by evaluating them honestly, that we can begin to arrive at insights into the mysteries of "Mother" that have historically been shrouded in the most cryptic of language and of graphic symbols. In other words, we move from inner conversation with our own mother to conversation with the archetypal Mother of mythologies and of world religions. Such transition of focus, and deepening, happens frequently in meditation.

THE EMPEROR

The Father

The Great Father thoughtfully administers a remote and harsh kingdom, the distant castle being symbolic of a process of reason so abstract that it has no object. In his right hand he holds a wand of creation (intentionally phallic), and in his left he holds a sword which may punish or destroy.

In Jungian psychology the Father is of lesser significance than is the Mother. Jung explained that this is because the mother is more important to the psychological formation of the child than is the father. However a woman might reasonably argue that Jung could only speak from the perspective of a man and that his observations of Animus (the female contrasexual component) was as an *outsider*. Certainly, Jung's descriptions of a father figure were not entirely objective. But the fact that his ideas were colored by a difficult relationship with his own father in no way detracts from the utility of his theories.

As we shall see in considering the 22 cards of the Major Arcana, the relationship between Mother and Son is philosophically primary. Yet, as this is largely symbolic description. The Mother nurtures the Son (the emerging self-consciousness), while the "Father" stands as guardian of the whole process. This is the most refined of symbolism. And until we can make it real, by applying it to the deepest, and often most repressed, feelings about our personal relationship to father and mother, the whole process can be, as Alice said, nothing more than a house of cards. Metaphysical symbolism is useless if not applied to real human problems and behavior. Consequently, we try to experience the *Emperor* as the very essence of Father in a real-life experience.

At the level of principle, *The Emperor* is the pure male which is the opposite of the pure female *Empress*. He represents outgoing force which inseminates, a martian energy which is restricted and acted upon by the formative female.

At the level of personal interaction and conversation, the father may be verbal, intellectual, and rational — sometimes to the point of being cold. And although he may inflict punishment, he is dynamically protective of his own. He is the provider of support, of strength, and of fatherly love. He is also the lawgiver although — as will be repeatedly underscored — the Father forgives, but the Mother does not. The opposite side of this Father figure is cruel, oppressive, and totally self-centered.

THE HIEROPHANT

The Father as Law-Giver

This is a difficult card relating to a Gnostic concept of *Demiurge* which supposes that the illusions of the material condition are created not by a Supreme Deity (God the Father) but by a Lesser Creator who (erroneously) believes himself to be Supreme. The crossed bands on his breast were, until recently, a sign of the Catholic priest's obedience to higher Church authority.

In the *Jungian Tarot* card, the Hierophant is seated on a throne, and is crowned with the triple tiara of a pope, as has become traditional. The Hierophant has often been related to the formal (i.e, restrictive) practices and authority of organized religion, "laws" that are often more arbitrary and culturally-determined than they are representative of universal truths. He is one who demands attention and respect, and who makes pronouncements with the absolute assurance that they are correct.

In *The Hierophant*'s right hand is a small figure representing Original Man (*The Lover*). This is the potentially perfected Self which will evolve within the restrictions of the earth − a condition created by the Hierophant.

From the standpoint of meditation and inner conversation, this is one of the most interesting cards of the deck. Generally it represents authority — an employer, a teacher, or some other figure in control. It may also mean a government, a person or body, which hands down laws controlling the individual and the society.

While *The Emperor* is the Father as *Law Maker*, *The Hierophant* is the Father as *Law Giver*. The distinction is an important one because, ultimately, the Hierophant is an administrator. He is an integral part of an organization. In other words, *The Emperor* works for himself; he is a creative free-agent. But *The Hierophant* works for a large organization whose rules he upholds strictly, although he is paradoxically unaware that this is the case.

The personality which we encounter may be variously benevolent and just, thoughtful and kind, or it may be high-handed, egocentric and even sadistic. We must deal with the Hierophant in whatever garb of temperament he may appear. By doing so, we work out our own relationship to authority. How do we feel about control in our lives? Do we resent those who atttempt to impose structure on us, feeling that it restricts our creative freedoms? Or do we need the psychological support of external regulation?

THE LOVER

Son as Collector of Experience

The Lover stands with arms outstretched above a male and a female figure. The Sun and the Moon behind him represent the two sexes as symbolic of dualities in manifestation. This is the *Magician*, at a lower level. *The Lover* is Original Man. He is, as was decribed for the earlier card, "author of Sun and Moon ...the source of all dualities and the means for their reconciliation."

As the Son in manifestation he is, by definition, bisexual, embodying both male and female principles. Jung points out that Christ (the Son as Perfected Self) is androgenous, having reconciled the tensions of sexual opposites. The same must be said of Buddha, Osiris, and all other "sacrificed gods."

Meditations with *The Lover* can be especially difficult because they may involve the direction of the waking consciousness toward the possibility of resolution with the unconscious, a condition of perception that has variously been described as the "Atman," the "Higher Self," the "Christ or Buddha within." Yet regardless of the way in which one may address this figure it is important to look beyond the assignment of sexuality as *male*. Perfected Self as male must not be taken as a social statement suggesting the superiority of one sex or another. This is all symbolic: male is the active, outgoing, creative principle and female is enclosing and acting upon that principle to produce a third. This may sound cold and distant, but meditation with the *Jungian Tarot* cards is unlikely to ever be an abstract, mathematical experience. Sparks fly quickly with each and every card that is touched upon.

Of course there are many legitimate means of approach to inner reality: emotional, intellectual, and devotional. One has the option of interaction with *The Lover* as an abstract principle or as an earthier *Animus*. But in any event, Self must be addressed at the individual level before it is possible to approach the more universal qualities of the Son as *Magician*.

Those who enjoy symbol-games might make a technical distinction, by referring *The Magician* as Animus/Anima to the Macrocosm, and *The Lover*, the Animus/Anima personal to each individual, to Microcosm. In this regard, the female figure in *Strength* is to the *Lover* as *High Priestess* is to *The Magician*. She is Anima. And again, ultimately Anima = Animus.

CHARIOT

The All-Present Father

The Chariot is perhaps the least understood card of the Tarot deck, one which can be explained only in terms of *The Hierophant* as Demiurge, i.e., as ruler over an illusory condition.

The principles involved, like so much that goes on in the magical world of the collective unconscious, is most easily expressed as a simple tale: The Hierophant, as we have seen, creates a world in which he claims absolute authority; he hides (whether intentionally, or in his own ignorance) from those living in this world, the fact that there is a Greater Father, to whom he is subject, and that the world over which he "rules" is a deception. It is into this imperfect world that the Son is born. But the Father, who is the Supreme Creator, provides his Son with a link to Himself, by which the Son may both be protected from the illusions of the Lessser Creator, and by which he may transcend that debased authority.

In terms of the Tarot, this is *The Chariot*, the Archetype of Spirit Below. The Charioteer is the only figure in the Tarot deck which can move between "planes," i.e., between states of consciousness, effortlessly. It is for this reason that the Chariot in the *Jungian Tarot* is not drawn by horses. It is, rather, propelled by the energy of the Crown, which is that of the Supreme Creator to whom, alone, the Charioteer is answerable. The Charioteer is also a helper which may be identified as the Guardian Angel.

In practical terms, it is understood that the Son represents the emerging self-consciousness. *The Chariot* is a card asserting that in this process we are not alone, and that there is inner guidance and protection which may lead us out of the illusion of our own sense perceptions. So how do we deal with the figure in meditation?

On one level this is the Father as protector. This is something of a *deus ex machina* figure − God lowered onto the medieval stage by a rope −. a figure who steps in to save the day when all else fails. Inner conversation logically begins with the figure as an aspect of our own father whose protection, good or bad, we consider. A meditation will then deepen to deal with what we have described as the relationship between the emerging Self, and the Supreme Creator which is the ultimate reality from which the self derives.

STRENGTH

The Daughter as Collector of Experience

Strength is the female aspect of *The Lover* separated out in the same way that the female aspect of *The Magician* is *The High Priestess*. As *The Lover* represents the Son, so *Strength* shows the Daughter. She is the consort of Original Man, who is represented in the upper right background. Together they will produce another Son within the confines of manifestation. The pattern of Mother/Father/Son is repeated over and over again.

Psychologically, this means that integration (the balance of opposites) takes place simultaneously at many levels of consciousness. The encounter of conscious and unconscious happens again and again, becoming ever more subtle until the "consciousness" is returned to the natural state of union symbolized in the Tarot by *The Fool*.

The card shows a young woman whose right hand rests upon the head of a lion — an image derived from apparent medieval Tarot references to *Leo*, which nineteenth century commentators expanded to mean control of sexual currents which have been called the *Kundalini*, or serpent energy. Indeed, innocence holding enormous

32

sexual power under control is a very appropriate explanation for this card.

Above her head are the stars, at her breast the Sun, and at her feet the Moon − a reference to the woman of the *Apocalypse*. But, in terms of that same text, she is also the Whore of Babylon. The obverse of this card, little understood, and never actually shown in a Tarot card is sexually unbridled, violent, brutal, even dangerous. Indeed, interaction with this archetype may be traumatic for some, because it requires a willingness to accept the psychological reality that brutality and barbarism always lurk beneath the most innocent human façade. Deeply-imbedded Christian faith may make it very difficult, or even impossible, for some readers to consider a dark opposite side to the Virgin Mary.

Woman, in every case (whether approached as Mother, Daughter, or Grandmother) relates to the underworld, as is suggested here by the steps heading downward, and by the cave at the feet of the *Empress*. This may lead to some very dark, undifferentiated, aspects of both the personal and the collective unconscious.

HERMIT

Grandfather as Teacher

The Hermit is at the edge of a desert which symbolizes a transition between conscious and unconscious, between darkness and the light of self-awareness. In his right hand he carries a lamp which will show the way across this terrible desert, a pilgrimage aptly described by St. John of the Cross as a "dark night of the soul." In his left hand he holds a staff set afire by a bolt of lightning from above. This is the magical staff of Moses, who led his people across the desert and out of bondage.

So the Hermit is teacher, and guide of souls, in which role he must be differentiated from the Hierophant and from the Charioteer. The Hierophant also teaches, but the law which he expounds is untrue; it obscures truth. The Charioteer is another who assists in the development of self-knowledge, but he is protector rather than guide or teacher. What must be kept in mind is that Hierophant, Charioteer, and Hermit are all aspects of the Father who, *in toto* is *The Emperor*.

The Wise Old Man archetype is the guide/teacher aspect of the Father which appears often in folk tales, such as the

34

Arthurian Legend in which he is Merlin. This is among the most ubiquitous of archetypes, one which fills a psychological need for most people. *The Hermit* is a comforting figure who encourages us onwards despite the odds, who lifts us gently when we occasionally fall, and who — most of all — knows what we do not. Here a point must be reiterated about the Father and Mother in their relationship to the Son (emerging self-consciousness of a man or of a woman): The Father forgives; the Mother does not. This is a principle which can only be understood through long experience of conversation with the archetypes.

As with all archetypes, the Wise Old Man has both a positive and a negative aspect. He is our personal Moses, the Thaumaturge who turns his staff into a serpent, or who parts the Red Sea and leads his flock to the promised land of Light. But he can also be the evil sorcerer — a vicious and cruel Hermit of the Rocks who delights in leading us astray and into danger.

WHEEL OF FORTUNE

The Mother
Who Determines Experience

The Wheel of Fortune has been generally accepted to mean fate, to mean chance and, especially, to mean good fortune — because of its traditional assignment to Jupiter, a broadly benevolent planet. Those who may not "believe" in astrology should at least be aware that the same medieval society which created Tarot, and which lacked a psychologically-descriptive vocabulary, often used planets to represent types of behavior and personalities. So, it may be assumed that the inventors of *The Wheel of Fortune* card intended that we interpret it in positive, Jupiterian, terms.

However in the *Jungian Tarot* deck, the emphasis on good fortune has been expanded to suggest a wide range of experience. Unlike the card's design in any previous deck, a female figure is shown behind a wheel to which a youthful male figure is attached. This represents one of the most significant contributions of Jungian psychology: it shows the Mother who determines the experience of the Son. In other words, as conscious and unconscious move closer together, toward the formation of something new (self-awareness, the Son), consciousness acts on the experiences generated by the unconscious.

Students of the history of art will immediately recognize Leonardo's design of a man in a circle, illustrating the Renaissance concept of man as "the measure of all things." At a personal level the small figure means each of us in transition; more broadly it is the ongoing experience of the human race itself.

The wheel is divided into 12 sections suggesting each of the signs of the zodiac as a discrete and different form of life experience. The principle is that the Mother determines the trials, pains, and pleasures of the Son by turning the *circle* which, in Jungian Psychology means *Self*. Twelve eyes around the circumference refer to the vision of Ezekial and thus relates *The Wheel of Fortune* to *The Chariot*.

For many, conversation with the Mother who is in control, may recall difficult and painful personal experience − haunting and unresolved vestiges of childhood which this figure will help to resolve.

JUSTICE

The Mother Who Punishes and Rewards

Justice is an aspect of the Mother who evaluates the progress of the Son and who administers rewards – or punishments that can be very harsh. The Mother is not forgiving; she gives the Son exactly what he has earned, no more and no less. In her left hand she holds a scale symbolic of her evaluation of the souls's progress; in her right hand she holds a sword which may either destroy or confer blessings (as in Knighthood).

It will be observed that this is the only card of the *Jungian Tarot* which shows an archetypal figure indoors. Justice takes place in a chapel-like environment, a space which is sanctified and is removed from the space of all other cards. Tarot commentators have, since the late nineteenth century, agreed that *Justice* should be conceptually isolated in some way. And, in fact, it has often been suggested that this card bears a very special relationship to *The Fool*, Archetype of Creative Spirit.

As a practical matter it is impossible to entirely separate the experience of *The Wheel of Fortune* from that of *Justice*. Indeed, conversation with one archetype may fade into the other very spontaneously. In *The Wheel of Fortune* the conversation is with the Mother who creates our experiences (some of which may appear totally arbitrary on her part), whereas in *Justice* we converse with the Mother who evaluates our performance in those experiences.

As we look back to some childhood task assigned by our mother, we may discover a deep sense of appreciation for her wisdom, or we may discover that we have repressed a great deal of hostility and must retread a path until some difficult materials have been resolved. The effort invokes a multitude of archetypal aspects of the mother.

Experience will demonstrate that lines between those many archetypes related to Mother, or to Father, are artificially drawn. In the natural pendulum swing from conscious to unconscious attention, the rules of the intellect are broken down whether we want them to be or not. In meditation, sense ultimately gives rise to perfect nonsense.

HANGED MAN

The Son Self-Sacrificed

The Hanged Man is the most curious image of the traditional Tarot deck and one for which esoteric and psychological interpretations have developed very slowly. Indications are that the card may originally have been meant to represent Judas hanging upside down and holding bags of silver. Insofar as the earliest cards appear to relate Gothic Humanism, and obviously allude to the "Virtues," it is quite possible that this figure was intended to represent the Vice of Avarice.

It was not until the eighteenth and ninteenth centuries that Tarot commentators began to attach to this card ancient myths of Gods hung in a Tree and subsequently resurrected.

Today *The Hanged Man* is generally agreed to represent a state of consciousnesss called *Sammahdi*, a Hindu word for which there is no western equivalent. It means a condition where the center of consciousness is reversed, and subject becomes object. One looks "down" from the unconscious to the conscious, rather than the other way around. In Christian terms this may be described as a mystical "Crucifixion in Space."

It is a psychological state wherein what we believe to be ourselves is completely "lost," (i. e., "sacrificed" to a greater principle). It is the logical consequence of enlightenment. So, this card represents *an action* of the Perfected Self. It is the Son who, having resolved the dualities of male and female, and who is the perfect product of interactive lessons of the mother and of the father, gives up all vestige of a personal self. Actually, *The Hanged Man* is but one aspect of the perfected Self; other aspects are represented by *The Magician*, by *The Lover* and by *The Sun*.

The *Jungian Tarot* card shows two centers of light, one above and one below, with the figure now rooted in the upper (unconscious) center. The design is intended to suggest that this condition results from interactive waves of thought and of experience — between the conscious and the unconscious, brought about through the use of the *Kundalini* force represented by the serpent coiled around the figure. The experience of this card may result from mental manipulation of sexual currents in the body, although casual experimentation is not recommended. Conversation with the *Hanged Man* invariably produces special insights and, some inevitable surprises — pleasant and unpleasant.

DEATH

The Mother as Gateway

It is unlikely that the medieval mind which invented this card intended that it be taken less than literally. In the fourteenth century Christian world, death was a condition of which people were constantly and coldly reminded. Indeed, today's idea that the *Death* card represents a transition indicates the extent to which the Tarot interepretation has evolved. In a modern climate, where the cards are analyzed in philosophical and in psychological terms, *Death* is popularly explained as showing a change from one condition to another; it is not considered to represent something final or absolute.

The *Jungian Tarot* version of *Death* requires some explanation, much of the symbolism being explicit to Jungian psychology. A figure of Death as the "Grim Reaper" holds in its left hand a scythe, and in its right an hour glass. He is walking across a bridge spanning dark and murky waters. And although the bridge is collapsing behind him to symbolize the end of a phase, it is certain that he will reach a new shore and a new beginning.

Behind the Death figure is a woman with arms outstretched. She is the passageway from one stage of consciousness to another, death in Jungian terms, being described as a return to the Mother. The black horse at the upper right also represents the Mother.

This card emphasizes again the significance of the Mother who bears the Son, who nurtures and teaches him, and to whom no matter what independence he may gain, he must return eventually.

Conversation should be with the hooded figure of Death, rather than with the background figure of the Mother — who may appear uninvited, and in very unexpected ways. Almost anything can happen in meditation with this card, which symbolizes the mystery of both birth and of death. Issues will emerge which we may either face directly or which we may subtly avoid by, among other ways, developing a conversation so intellectual and abstract that it denies the issue of mortality. Most important here is that we address our own feelings about overwhelming transitions, of which death is only one.

TEMPERANCE

The Conciliatory Daughter

It may be legitimately argued that the figure in *Temperance* is androgenous. Indeed, most decks show this figure as an angel rather than as a human personality. But in *The Jungian Tarot* the archetypal image is that of a young girl, to suggest the importance of absolute innocence (lack of prejudice) in the active and ongoing process represented here.

The card depicts a ritual: On a natural stone "altar" water is poured onto fire, and fire is immersed in water, meaning that one opposite is tempered, or mediated by the other. The twelve candles in the background suggest twelve signs of the zodiac which, in psychological terms, symbolize the variety and totality of human experience. The principle is far reaching and practical. Within the context of any given experience, we learn to *consciously* bring opposites into play.

At the most simplistic level this can mean "counting to ten" when we are angry yet want to avoid doing something rash. Or it can mean counting our blessings when everything seems to be going wrong.

44

At a more subtle level this is the invocation of another point of view, such as that of the official "Devil's advocate" who, in the Catholic religion, argues the faults of a candidate for sainthood. In debate with ourselves we learn to neutralize the emotional or intellectual significance of any situation, and to see as an observer. This card helps us to recognize that there are dualities in everything, and that we function in pendulum swings from happy to sad, from love to hate, from thoughtful to emotional.

At a third, and most refined level, this card refers to a wave interaction of those positive and negative sexual energies consciously manipulated within the body through Yoga, or through certain little-understood Christian and Jewish meditational exercises. The process has been described in the past using alchemical and other symbolic terms. Today such nomenclature has been supplanted by psychological language provided by pioneers such as Freud, Jung, Adler, and Erkison. Moreover science has begun to accurately measure some of the effects of meditation and "mind control" on the body, including actual physiochemical changes.

THE DEVIL

The Dark Son

In the *Jungian Tarot*, two of the trumps are of identical design: *The Lover* and *The Devil*. These represent opposite aspects of the same principle. And insofar as *The Devil* is the dark side of Original Man, it might be called the most important card of the entire Tarot. Whereas *The Lover* is a Christ (as metaphor of Perfected Self) figure, *The Devil* is the *Anti-Christ*. In this regard it will be seen that in the mandala of *The Lover* the fish (a symbol of Christ) points counter-clockwise, meaning return to the Godhead; that on *The Devil* card points clockwise toward manifestation, i.e. toward the earth.

It should be understood that although exoteric Christianity has found little of value in the dark aspects of things, what has been called "evil" is absolutely essential to the process of individuation. There can be no light without darkness; there can be no Christ without an Anti-Christ; there can be no resolution of the dualities of consciousness without encounter of the black waters of discord.

The attribution of this card to Capricorn, the sign of cardinal earth, is very appropriate since *The Devil* represents enslavement of consciousness by the illusion of matter. And one must be immersed in the material condition to this extreme before release is possible.

The idea is expressed in Christian allegory as Christ facing the tests of Satan and descending to the depths of hell. The principle is symbolized in alchemy as the blackness and decay from which gold emerges. And the fact that this theme has been expressed in so many ways throughout history makes clear that different cultures have been symbolizing the same important psychological (and archetypal) process.

The experience of conversation with this figure may, initially, prove difficult. The Devil, as a key archetype of the collective unconscious, is unquestionably irrational — generating anxiety. It will be found somewhat less stressful to deal with the figure as Archetype of Shadow, which embodies (generally speaking) the most negative and inferior qualities of our own personalities.

THE TOWER

The Father as Avenger/Protector

The Tower is one of the *Jungian Tarot* cards in which a figure has been added to the usual design. The image of the Martial Father is so perfectly logical here that this picture may be argued to be a restoration of a deeply-buried archetypal image, rather than merely an artistic embellishment. Of course, as has been stated repeatedly, it is impossible to be certain about the meanings intended for each Trump by the originators of the cards. But, over the centuries, artists have (consciously or unconsciously) been bringing these designs ever closer to those collectively agreed-upon images which Jung called the Archetypes of the Collective Unconscious.

This card has been called one of destruction and of physical death; it has been related to the North, "place of greatest darkness" from which light emerges, meaning that every end is a new beginning. It has also been called "The House of God," to imply that spiritual learning involves the absolute destruction of old concepts and of old ways of life. *The Tower* could not be called a card of pleasant experience.

But an interpretation of this figure as the Father who protects and avenges points toward the positive aspects of radical change. Conversation with the father in this card may act as a corrective to what some have felt to be an overemphasis by Jung on the role of the Mother.

The figure behind *The Tower* is The Emperor who has stepped down from his exalted throne, and has donned armor. His task is to sweep away institutions that have become useless in our lives. A sword in one hand destroys utterly, but the other hand holds a rose of peace and conciliation.

As with all of the cards, there is a personal and a collective lesson. We may converse with a father who has made a major and unpleasant decision, such as to demand that we move out of his house, or to inflict a severe and sudden punishment about which we had been previously warned. And this is a card forcing us to consider the source of negative life experiences such as loss of job, illness and other disasters which seem to arbitrarily befall us. Are there accidents or do we we reap what we sow? These are questions to be addressed directly to this achetypal image.

THE STAR

The Virgin Daughter

The Star is among the most dynamic of the archetypes with which to converse. It is a magical figure which is simple and beautiful. It is the essence of inspiration. The Maiden is the Empress who has descended from her exalted realm and entered a new state of innocence. She will eventually be the consort of the Hero-Son, who now struggles in search of her on his Path toward the independence of Self-awareness.

Language falls very short in its attempt to describe the energies involved here. Only through highly refined intuition can one approach *The Star*. This Maiden who is the essence of inspiration for the Hero, is a very real condition of consciousness which has been called *Sol Invisibilis* (the "Hidden Sun"), and the *Lumen naturae* (the "Light of Nature"), among other descriptive terms.

Throughout history, visionaries (actually the earliest psychologists), have attempted to describe conditions of consciousness such as that represented by this card. And, unquestionably, the writings of the illuminatii of societies past is of inestimable value. Yet, we must exercise discrimination about those reports. Whereas many descriptive terms in the mystical literature are entirely symbolic (meaning that they point toward something beyond the senses); other terms, though often thought to be symbolic, mean exactly what they say. Such is is the case with *The Star* as Sol Invisibilis. This is an inner light, a sort of central point of brilliance, which anyone can easily experience by simply closing their eyes and "looking" for it.

The qualities of this inner light are those of *The Star*. It is loving, inspirational, and totally irrational. In symbolic terms, it is that into which the emerging Self is born; it is both guide and gateway. The gold and silver pitchers merge different aspects of consciousness, returning them to the primordial pool from which they originally came.

To converse with this figure as an ideal image of female innocence is not difficult, and may provide both men and women useful insights into this aspect of their own personality structures. But to work effectively with the archetype as the Inner Light, requires experience with meditation. As usual, one asks repeated questions. But responses may be especially cryptic, or even absurd, and the experienced meditator will "feel" rather than taking anything at face value. It is difficult to explain, for example, that this "Star" is not one, but many in one.

THE MOON

Grandmother:
The Deadly Mother

This card is among those which has been most radically modified in terms of Jungian psychology. The woman here is something of a "missing link" archetype that has, previously, only been implied. The Moon is all phases of woman at once — Diana and Hecate. But in Tarot the bright side of the Moon, such as that found in *The High Priestess* or in *The Star*, has been traditionally emphasized. So, the introduction of the personality of the hag as the Moon's darkest qualities is useful.

The Moon carries some of the most important lessons of the Tarot. It is the card to which earlier centuries ascribed witchcraft and magic spells; in modern psychological terms, this means deception, phantoms of our own creation, and deep-rooted fears which seem to well up out of nowhere. This is a card of the deepest anguish and inner pain. This is also a card of childbirth.

For a woman the experience of this archetype is extremely difficult; for an intellectual man it may seem almost impossible. This is that dark side of the Mother which a woman may intuitively understand, but which a man would strive to avoid at all costs. This is the Archetype of the Deadly Mother, the figure recognized in most mythologies as the Wicked Witch. She is a frightening spectre.

The Deadly Mother is an archetype which can only be known in its relationship to the Son as emerging Self-consciousness. It is she who imposes the most dangerous trials, who throws out tests that may destroy. She imposes a mantle of deep sorrow and of phantoms which may be overcome only be recognizing them for what they really are − illusions.

The card pictures the Deadly Mother as Hecate, whose arms indicate that she is the goddess of crossroads. Behind her are both Sun and Moon, but the light of the Sun has been obscured; truth has been clouded over. Below the figure, lower forms emerge from a sea of menstrual blood. At the card's center a tiny figure has braved the wolves and has reached the topmost step where he is fearlessly confronting the Dark Mother within himself.

There is a definite relationship between *The Moon* and *Death*, which has been described as a return to the mother. Here, too, is a purposeful return to the womb of consciousness. But the Hero will return to the earth reborn. Recalling that the Mother rules the Underworld, it will be recognized that this means the descent into hell.

THE SUN

The Child

The Sun is the center of our physical solar system; it is the source of light and of life. Symbolically, it is the Prince who rules (in the name of his Father/King) over the material condition. Now the Child archetype represents this Prince as he begins to know the boundaries of the Kingdom which he administers. The Child represents the early stages of true self-consciousness, the conscious mind encountering and conquering the contents of the unconscious. And the Child represents what will be. He is a *numinous* and magical figure with roots in the deepest past, and although he exists in the present, he is the future of the individual consciousness and, in fact, that of the consciousness of the human race.

Encounter of the Divine Boy, the Young God, may be an extraordinary meditative experience, particularly insofar as the work requires genuine control of irrational (dream quality) materials.

The most obvious point about the Child is that he does not yet stand entirely apart from his parents. The Father, and the Mother, continue to provide. The Mother shapes

54

the character and experiences of the Child/Hero, pushing him toward independence. The Father, on the other hand, protects, shelters, and supplies food during the early period of development (For the mature young man, the Father will become teacher).

The real meaning of the Father/Mother/Child symbolism in mythologies and in religions begins to be apparent in conversation with the archetype of this card. Self-consciousness, an understanding of the true meaning of life, is the result of a "unification" of opposites. This Self-Consciousness — symbolic Child — emerges from a perfect integration of the Conscious (Father) and the (Mother) Unconscious.

The Archetype of the Child is central to many other Archetypes. *The Sun* is another of those cards filled with surprises and which has, as do all archetypes, some very dark aspects. Indeed, the chief task of the Child/Hero is the overcoming of darkness through the inner sunlight.

JUDGMENT

The Son Who Judges

There are two common areas of confusion about this card. The first has to do with the difference between it and the card of *Justice*; the second has to do with the concept of "Last Judgment."

Justice represents the evaluation of a specific event or performance for which one may be rewarded or punished as part of an ongoing learning process. This may be within the context of daily experience, or it may be an aspect of spiritual development. The Mother rewards the child for good behavior, and punishes for bad behavior. In psychological terms, this means that *we reward and punish ourselves*. The *Justice* perspective comes into play when we look critically at something we have done and feel comfortable with success or disturbed by mistakes. Our self-criticism in a given situation repeats over and over again, as does the very real and very specific reward or punishment which we bring to ourselves.

But *Judgment* is a different matter. It represents an evaluation at the end of a long cycle, such as retirement from a job, end of a marriage, graduation from college, completion of a book, or a building, or some lengthy project. It is, in many respects, a "Last Judgment." But that term is misleading, since we experience the end of cycles over and over again. Thus, this card represents the Archetype of Rebirth. It shows a pause, a momentary turning inward and looking back, before the beginning of something entirely new.

In the most profound sense, this card describes an interim report on the progress of the soul toward "liberation", an assessment of the extent to which the unity of opposing "male" and "female" (here being resurrected, i.e., raised up for judgment) principles has taken place. There is no punishment or reward as most would understood those terms (and as definitely happens within the framework of the card of *Justice*). The Judgment declares whether, on a variety of levels, one is free or remains shackled by unresolved unconscious materials. That is the true "Salvation" or "Damnation," as Christianity has labeled the process. Both are (temporary) conditions of consciousness resultant from self-scrutiny.

THE WORLD

The Daughter
Who Conceals Herself

Persona is a latin word meaning "mask" and referring especially to the masks worn in the Greek and Roman theatre. In Jungian terms the Persona is the mask which we show to the world, the outer personality by which we are known. Our lives are not unlike a play in which we hide our true faces under masks, and in which we know others primarily by the masks which they wear. In the card the dancing figure whose face is hidden is that of Anima. We understand that Persona is an aspect of Anima, Persona being the outer self and Anima is the inner. One is the opposite of the other: Those who project aloofness and rationality tend to be more irrational and affectionate inside.

On the other hand, an emotional individual will usually have a very rational Anima.

Of course, Persona is only one of the many significant archetypes involved here. This card is entitled *The World* (rather then *The Universe* as it is in many decks) because it represents all of the elements of the material condition. And one can only admire the unknown medieval symbolist who originally devised this remarkably rich and concise symbolic image.

The material condition was considered to be a compendium of four elements: Fire, Water, Air, and Earth — all of which were activated by a fifth element, Spirit. On the card the Lion is Fire, the Eagle is Water, the Man is Air, and the Ox is Earth. The figure of Anima appears within a "uroboros," meaning eternity (and related to *The Magician* — Mercurius — of which Animus is the female aspect). The dancing figure, an extremely powerful and significant archetype in itself, is the wave action of Spirit activating matter.

A discussion of the symbolism of the card may sound rather poetic, if not distant, but the image describes a profound and practical activity on a multitude of levels. One of the catch phrases of Western mysticism is "as above, so below." In this regard, *The World* contains all of the elements that were unexpressed in *The Magician*. Here is the totality of the individual in a world where opposites are expressed with the greatest polarity. The card describes the waking consciousness, and the mechanisms of the public self, the Persona, which each individual develops to deal with society.

KING OF WANDS

The Aggressive Father

The Aggressive Father is a man of great force and independence who says exactly what he thinks — all too often without concern for the feelings of others — and who has the utmost belief in his own abilities. He is a pioneer, one who is masterful, independent, and self reliant. He is a dynamic and intuitive personality who insists on being in charge, and who quickly sees solutions to problems. He is a sympathetic person who, surprisingly, feels that he is not himself understood. And it is true that he may live in a creative mental world unknown to others.

The King of Wands can be a wonderful and caring father, a source of constant adventure and learning, of whom the child is very proud. But he can also be very difficult, tending to make irrational and impulsive demands of everyone around him; he can be impatient, domineering, and embarrassingly eccentric. Sometimes the child feels put off by this father who sets such a high standard in all that he does. The child understands that reward or punishment comes swiftly from this man.

The outgoing and creative qualities of the Aggressive

Father may be exciting or they may be abrasive. The very least that can be said of this man as a father is that he is never boring!

QUEEN OF WANDS

The Stylish Mother

The Stylish Mother is a woman of great intelligence. She is strong-willed, sensitive and quite ambitious, a woman who wants to be the center of attention — and who usually is. Hers is a magnetic and charming personality, a stylish presence to be felt the moment she enters a room. She is very witty, a master of language whose words are always subtle and amusing, but whose quips can ruthlessly devastate one who has crossed her in some way. She may be warm, outgoing, and inspiring of adoration, but her moods swing rapidly. She will quickly anger, and then just as quickly forgive and forget.

She is a freewheeling idealist, is very intuitive, and loves to impose her creative will on the people and things around her. And she feels deeply, although that may not be obvious to strangers, with whom she may be very aloof, and to whom she usually presents a polished mask. She is actually far more vulnerable than most people realize. Her sometimes "bitchy" attitude can be very self-protective; her independence and outgoing qualities are deeply based in the security of her family environment. She loves her home and ferociously protects her children from what she perceives as a hostile and unsophisticated outside world.

PRINCE OF WANDS

The Affectionate Son

This is a thoughtful and observant young man, a good judge of people and of situations who finds it difficult to make cautious decisions; he usually acts before he thinks. His greatest strength is a finely-tuned sensitivity to the feelings of those around him — especially insofar as those feelings affect him directly. He can be a caring and devoted friend who inspires affection as easily as he gives it. He loves to be in love, although he may be very fickle; he hates to be tied down to anyone or anything for very long.

He is basically independent, but dislikes being alone.

He enjoys being surrounded by many different people — who find him to be affectionate, outgoing and friendly. He loves the distraction of games, of parties, of art, and of beautiful things. The Affectionate Son is not an emotionally secure person, and, in a bad situation, may become pathologically dependent upon others. He may also have a very strong attachment to his mother.

He is an intelligent but undisciplined youth who would rather engage in play than in reading or in anything that requires long periods of concentration. He is a daydreamer, a romantic who is sometimes off in a fantasy world of his own creation.

PRINCESS OF WANDS

The Clever Daughter

Although this young woman appears very outgoing, she is actually insecure and vulnerable. Nothing matters to her more than to be surrounded by people and to be in a social spotlight. She seeks constant attention and emotional support, and uses her very considerable guile to twist people to her point of view. She is remarkably clever though not overly intelligent. And although she can be warm and loving, she can also be cruel — sometimes tearing people down behind their backs and ridiculing those who do not live up to her standards.

Always acting on impulse, she can be extraordinarily imaginative and witty — to the delight of those around her. But she is subject to intense swings in personality: one moment she is the soul of decorum and the next is genuinely vulgar. She behaves according to what will bring her attention at any given moment. Most find her unpredictability very amusing, but a few are very irritated by her behavior which they consider immature.

She is usually a center of attention, but at those rare times when she is alone, she may feel depressed and hostile. She derives a certain security from possessions, and loves to shop, but is not really attached to material things.

ACE OF WANDS

Birth and Death

This is a card of dynamic new beginnings, of things which have never been before. The change is overwhelming and revolutionary, and — whether voluntary or involuntary — it affects everything as it has been known. In the most literal and absolute sense, this may mean birth or death. It may also mean a new profession, a new home and new friends in a distant city, or a financial loss or gain which forces a new lifestyle.

This is not a card for the faint-hearted. It is a card of action and of confrontation which may be exhilarating or which may be devastating. The *Ace of Wands* brings passionate, transforming, energy into play.

Raw power, tremendous outgoing force, is unbridled here, either for the individual, or for a society. What is suggested is the root energy of life itself and the effect of its movement. It may cause an intense struggle leading to the start of significant advancement for the individual. Or, in society, it may cause the birth or fall of nations, such as occurred during the French and American revolutions. This may also mean the emergence of a totally new set of concepts about art, literature, government, or religion.

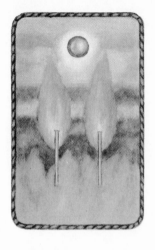

TWO OF WANDS

Invention

Whereas the Aces, generally, suggest something very abstract, the twos through tens represent more specific actions, experiences, and states of consciousness. The *Two of Wands* means creative inventiveness expressed boldly, even rashly. An idea emerges that is absolutely brilliant and original — the product of a tremendously free, intelligent and independent mind. A person insists on doing things their own way, refusing to be channeled by anyone or by any organization. The "inventor" is totally immersed in the work, to the extent that such single-mindedness may be very irritating to others.

By definition, the inventor has little support, since there is no precedent (like Edison's invention of the light bulb) for the effort. But dedication and unshakable belief in a project brings results of pure brilliance. Interestingly enough, as history has demonstrated with inventions of the greatest importance, the name of the inventor may be lost or obscured.

Meditation with this card, immersion in the principle of pure invention, may be a very useful experience. Approached properly, this card will allow anyone to touch (at least lightly) upon the essence of creative genius.

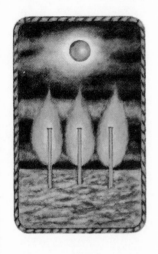

THREE OF WANDS

Fantasy

The *Three of Wands* means fantasy and mystery. It involves feelings which, at the most refined level, are "without object," and which may be intensified for either good or evil. There is here a subtle yet powerful flow — like the unseen undercurrent of an apparently peaceful river.

This is a card of intuition, of mysticism, of religion, and of the occult. It suggests deeply hidden currents of controlling energy within the collective unconscious. Indeed, this is a card of collective energy as opposed to that of the individual. It may, thus, be taken to depict the loss of individuality into something greater — a positive growth experience if it happens consciously. On the other hand, this may be a card of total madness if the fantasy materials are uncontrolled and impose on the waking consciousness. This is the key to *active imagination*, and meditation on it may be, as the old Hermetic axiom said, a process of "watching the watcher."

Insofar as this Three represents a collection of archetypes of transformation, it may also mean *travel* for its own sake, or it may mean an outpouring of benevolence and charity.

FOUR OF WANDS

Success

The success of the *Four of Wands* is largely a result of personal ability and of driving ambition. Here is a true innovator, a pioneer whose sincerity and honesty in his or her work earns the respect and admiration of everyone. However, this is not a card of creative genius as is *The Two of Wands*. Rather it is one of earnest endeavor and of resultant rewards.

The card suggests a plan carefully laid and brought into being through great enthusiasm, strength, and inspiration. This could mean religious inspiration, or it could mean a social, political, or even artistic cause of some sort.

The person is intelligent, self-assured (tending toward

egocentricity) and is occasionally very pig-headed. Once the mind is made up, there is no changing direction, a fact which may potentially lead to emotional, physical, or financial stress. Projects of *The Four of Wands* are never entirely without risk, although most often they turn out favorably. There is always the possibility that the push of energy required here will be too forceful, that resources will be severely overextended, and that loss of money or profession may result.

FIVE OF WANDS

Assertiveness

The Five of Wands is another of those cards representing a quality of behavior that may be applied for any purpose whatsoever, good or bad. It is a card of *action*, of assertiveness, of combativeness, and of originality. It is not a card of results, as is *The Four of Wands*, rather, it is a card of process without regard to outcome. The card may mean great personal courage, such as risking one's life to save another, or putting a reputation on the line for something in which one sincerely believes. It may mean

69

popularity and considerable success through one's own efforts. At best this is a card of candor, of clearly and emphatically expressed decision. However, this is a card of action, not of thought, and a decision is likely to be reached quickly.

Impulsivenesss and rashness may cause problems: Creative energy may be rapidly dissipated. At its most negative, the action here is very thoughtless − an aggressive attack or warring behavior. As anyone who has ever been subject to a demanding superior will attest, there is a thin line between intelligently assertive management, and management which is arbitrary and tyrannical.

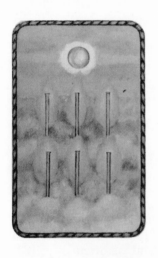

SIX OF WANDS

Strong Leadership

Although qualities of administration are related to many cards of the Tarot, *The Six of Wands* is the key card of leadership in the deck. The person tends to be head-strong and impulsive, a self-assured and somewhat egocentric individual who easily assumes command under any circumstances, and who handles difficult situations with skill.

The man or woman loves challenge, and may be somewhat reckless. There is a combination of strength and spontaneity; one is always ready for a new adventure or for a good fight. The more fierce the competition the better.

There is tremendous loyalty and caring for subordinates, who are dealt with thoughtfully and with concern for their opinions, and who return these feelings with affection and with sincere trust.

Of course, there is good and there is bad leadership. A less than ideal administrator may deceive or lie to subordinates. He or she may be insensitive to the feelings of others, or concerned only with the job at hand. At the very worst, a person may exercise control in ways which are violent and aggressive.

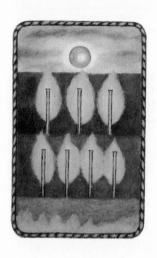

SEVEN OF WANDS

Passion

The infatuation of this card is overwhelming, but it burns out quickly. Indeed "Passion" is not, by definition, enduring. It is a temporary imbalance of feelings which determines action until reason, or a more cautious overview, turns the pendulum back toward reason.

There may be a powerful sexual attraction or a hasty marriage. Or the card may represent an attraction to painting or to music without sufficient discipline to create anything really worthwhile. There may be great love of beautiful things, of style, or clothes, or jewelry. On the other hand, although glamour and luxury are seductive, they are ultimately found to have little substance.

The energies of this card are exciting. Love and money may come like a tidal wave, but be wasted. There is here the possibility of loss of love, money, or friends, through one's own excesses.

This is a card by which we learn to "watch the watcher," by which we analyze the very essence of our inmost desires. It helps us to consider the nature of raw passion, desire which can control us if we are not careful.

EIGHT OF WANDS

Intellectual Activity

In this Eight the dynamic and aggressive qualities of Wands, the "Fire" suit, is applied to intellect. There is a rapid rush of ideas, expressed in literary activities of all kinds, such as books, articles, public speaking, and criticism. Writing of high quality may be produced quickly. The work may be of great originality or even of true genius.

But, as with all Wands, the results of the push forward depend upon the person and the circumstances. Most important, the inspiration needs to be "brought down to earth." Unstructured ideas must be organized into clear form or they will dissipate. Without organization, the sparks of inspiration may come to nothing: speech may be rash; consequences may be ill-considered.

Writers understand deeply what is involved here. It is the translation of unconscious materials into the linear and sequential perceptions of the conscious mind. It is as if a work pre-exists somewhere *in toto* and is brought down to reality by the writer. This process is not an easy one; if it were, great poets, novelists, and philosophers would abound in society.

73

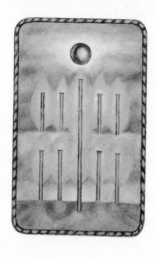

NINE OF WANDS

Anger

This is a card of raw emotion. It represents volatility and irrational impulse – anger which may dissipate as quickly as it appears. It may mean egocentric changeability and childish temper tantrums of the worst sort, springing forth when some inner nerve is struck.

The flash of anger brings with it a temporary loss of self-control, perhaps pointing toward deeply unresolved inner tensions. Generalized hostility toward one's environment, family, friends and co-workers, may, in fact, be the first indication of emotional disturbance. In more specific terms, the card may mean potentially threatening plots and secrets, or it may suggest a scandal which suddenly "explodes."

The *Nine of Wands* shows a fiery and potentially very dangerous instability. An important lesson is that even those who appear to be the best balanced have within them unconscious, primitive, feelings which may erupt to the surface without warning. Those who appreciate this, and who do not deny the existence of such feelings, are best equipped to function in a society of civilized "masks."

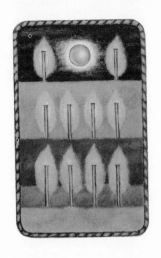

TEN OF WANDS

Control over Others

The Ten of Wands shows the careful and deliberate management of a structured group of people — generally a large organization. This is a card of great structure, of careful plan and of control. But the leadership is not generalized (as it is in the *Six*, the card of "Strong Leadership"). Rather it functions only within the context of a given organization. Expressed in another way: one may become the head of a vast empire by being a financial wizard or an organizational genius, not necessarily by being the natural leader implied by the *Six*.

Although the *Ten of Wands* means success through large companies and organizations, it also points to the isolation, and occasionally lonliness, of being at the pinnacle of authority.

The exercise of power and control over others is usually strong, well-reasoned, and self-assured. But occasionally the card may show defensiveness and irritability resulting when a plan turns out to be badly organized and diffuse.

KING OF CUPS

The Intellectual Father

The Intellectual Father lives in a world of thought which separates him from most of those around him. His mind is amazingly agile, and darts from one creative idea to another with ease. He is highly introspective, sensitive, and intuitive, but may hold concepts about himself which are unrealistic. He often believes that he is misunderstood and needs constant sympathy, understanding, and love.

He feels warmth and affection toward people but is critical of the abilities and performance of others, and finds it painful to accept shortcomings in those whom he loves. He finds it difficult, for example, to punish his beloved children.

This man is a daydreamer who may show little of himself openly. No matter how candid and honest he may appear to be, there are secret parts of himself that he can never quite share. Nevertheless, he operates remarkably well in society, being able to detach himself from ideals and function in a routine, which makes him a very good businessman.

At times he may be rebellious and impulsive, and may

cause problems for others. At an extreme — if pressures make him somehow unable to cope — he may withdraw into a world of fantasy.

QUEEN OF CUPS

The Emotional Mother

This is a highly emotional and sensitive woman. She is affecionate but self-protective, a quality which makes her appear somewhat unapproachable. She does not easily let people into her world yet, although it is difficult for her to entirely trust others, she can be the most loyal of friends. She can also be a person who is great fun, intensely charming and entertaining, one who senses the right thing to say at the right time.

And she has a strong moral character, a sense of right and wrong, and of order, which tends to keep her emotional personality under control, and which helps her to compensate for a certain lack of self-confidence. She does not soon forgive those who break the rules; she dislikes behavior which she considers thoughtless and inappropriate. She is very domestic, loves home, and tends to be somewhat overprotective of her children. Outside of the home, her natural suspiciousness makes her a very shrewd businesswoman. Physical beauty, luxury, and material objects are important in her life, and she knows how to get them.

At her worst she may be brooding, suspicious, defensive, and very erratic in her behavior.

PRINCE OF CUPS

The Charming Son

This Prince is a very charming, emotional, and romantic young man who enjoys being a center of attention, who can be truly delightful with a group of people, and who is usually subtle, sparkling, witty, and diplomatic. He receives a great deal of attention and is constantly being pursued — which has tended to make him rather self-centered and superficial in his interactions. He gives very little of himself which, perhaps ironically, is part of his attraction.

He is a very detached observer of people (whom he

often uses to his own advantage) but his judgments are usually quite subjective; he sees people in his own terms and can be quite thoughtless about the feelings of others. He is capricious and elusive in relationships, but although he likes to "play around" is actually a very loving person. He can be a wonderful friend to someone who places no strictures on his behavior.

This is an idealist who is afraid of being hurt and who avoids conflict, although he may generate considerable friction without intending to do so. He loves music and art and, although he has some talent at painting and at writing, would rather let others expend the creative effort.

PRINCESS OF CUPS

The Ambitious Daughter

Here is a very practical and ambitious young woman with natural executive skills for business. She is extremely calculating and shrewd, but is sensitive to the feelings of people around her. She easily earns the friendship and respect of business colleagues.

Keen insight into her own behavior and into that of others, makes her a remarkably good manager of employees or of those subordinate to her in any situation. She is a force to be reckoned with at a bargaining table. Her terms may be very demanding and, although she knows exactly when a compromise is to her advantage, she is not easily backed down. Yet she remains feminine and charming at all times.

She rarely causes dissention or ill-will, and maneuvers easily around petty jealousies and "office politics." When problems do occur, it is often due to a failure on her part to communicate clearly.

She needs (and gets) a great deal of affectionate support, but is not especially family-oriented. She may marry and have children, but her work always come first, a fact which may cause misunderstanding and separation from those whom she loves most.

ACE OF CUPS

Change of Feelings

This is the most emotional card of the deck and one of the most powerful of the Minor Arcana. Suggested here is an emotional upheaval whereby new feelings are substituted for old. Such new feelings at once challenge and transform. As the emotions swing radically from one point to another, there is a concomitant and equally strong change at all levels. Feeling, in this case, precedes the structure of thought or of action.

In the individual this may mean a turnabout in emotions toward another person, or it may mean a total reversal of values. In society, such values in conflict may mean the passion of a new religion, or of a new political movement. The card represents a tremendous outpouring of group energy to effect change.

The fact that a profound change in feelings has been responsible for something new may not be obvious. What goes on here tends to transcend external appearances and, most certainly, is related to activity within the collective unconscious. The *Ace of Cups* is really that pure and objectless root of emotion which touches upon great mysteries and deep secrets.

TWO OF CUPS

Adventure

As the adventure card of the Tarot, the *Two of Cups* represents a very wide range of situations and conditions outside of ordinary day-to-day existence and, to some extent, beyond the control of the individual. The (usually chosen) experience may be travel to an unknown land, visiting new places, and experiencing new customs, foods, and behavior. It may be a brief, possibly sexual, encounter. A situation may be planned, or it may be an exhilarating and challenging surprise.

There are two considerations: First, a great heightening of sensation; feelings are unusually sensitive. And second, there is no security in this unpredictable experience, which may be exciting and safe, but which could also be dangerous and mean trouble at home or in the workplace. As in any adventure, there is no certainty about what may happen next, or about how the situation will be resolved.

Moreover, the "adventure" is specific to each person and to their past experience. To a lion tamer a safari may be routine, whereas to an librarian it may be the event of a lifetime. In general, this card means an exciting change from routine.

THREE OF CUPS

Secure Environment

This card is the opposite of the *Two*. The *Three of Cups* is a card meaning protective home environment, a situation where all essential needs are met and where there is physical and emotional security. The card suggests well-being and a very protected, enclosed place. This is usually, though not always, the protection of a family unit, and often involves a very close association with the mother. Indeed (and in the best symbolic sense) mother *is* home. She is the womb to which one may return-although not without the payment of some dues.

The home is a center of strength, a space into which one may safely withdraw, that gives nourishment for life's fray outside of the walls. This is a card of nurture, of sympathy and of stylish refinement which may be charming and comforting but which, when taken to an extreme, becomes decadence.

A "secure environment" may be a blessing, or it may be a prison. The responsibilities of home may become oppressive, and a person may react to this pressure with escapist behavior, by a retreat from reality or even, as a final resort, by leaving the old home for a new one.

FOUR OF CUPS

Benevolence and Pleasure

The experience here is one of comfort, of charity, of kindness, and of very good humor. Amusing companionship, fine food and drink abound. Parties, dinners, and entertainments may seem endless. Whatever one wishes seems to be provided.

Sensitivity is expanded. The imagination is filled with new ideas which are easily expressed through painting, through music and through poetry. Some excellent work may result, but what goes on is not so much creative inspiration as it is a deluge of stimuli.

As with the *Three*, there is a protective home linked especially to the mother, who makes every effort to maintain and to improve its security. There may also be considerable financial ease. The mother or her family may, in fact, provide a great deal of money either through gift or through inheritance. The card may also refer to pleasurable travel by water (the element symbolically associated with mother).

The negative possibilities of this card relate to the potential extremes of pleasure. This may mean overindulgence leading to obesity, hangovers, and perhaps becoming jaded and bored by constant stimulation.

FIVE OF CUPS

Troubles

This card represents some of the most difficult and painful of human experiences. It means trouble of all sorts, and perhaps a lingering and incurable illness. There may be ill-will, lies, slander, theft, and scandal of the worst kind. There may be tremendous indecision; a person may be almost dangerously subject to the influence and whims of others.

The negative possibilities are very broad and include the risk of drowning, of scalding, and of poisons in food. The card may also indicate an escape into occultism and mysticism.

These are serious difficulties but (as opposed to the *Ten*), problems are almost entirely of one's own making. In this regard it should be noted that Cups, the suit of Water, is usually related to the unconscious. So this card may be interpreted as the fulfillment of an unconscious desire for the negative experience.

Such interpretation may lead to the philosophical principle of self-determination, the postulate that the experience of each individual is a matter of personal choice at some essential level, although the mechanisms of such choice may not be evident to the waking consciousness.

SIX OF CUPS

Sympathetic Attachment

This is among the most useful of the Tarot cards with which to meditate. It relates to care for family or for some special association. The group is of far greater importance than the individual, who perceives purpose only in terms of service to that group. The individual is submerged in the collective mind of others to the extent that self-reliance may disappear and be replaced by reliance on the group. This may represent an important phase, as in the case of teenagers who seek out peer support, or it may constitute a problem.

Attachment to external things, to people and to possessions, is very strong. Relationships are deeply felt, and there is sincere concern for the feelings of others. There is also a strong attachment to material objects, which may bring with them a sense of "roots" and of security.

This may be a very positive card, one of selfless dedication which earns the reward of protection from the group which is served. But, taken to an extreme, there may be moodiness and withdrawal from needed friends and loved ones. There is here, the potential for somewhat masochistic behavior.

SEVEN OF CUPS

Obstacles

The card of obstacles relates most commonly to personal interactions and to finances (i.e., to love and to money) areas in which being somehow "blocked" can be the most stressful. The activity here may be very subtle and, often, involves one or both parents. This is not a card of independence from home, although it may mean family strife and even a serious clash over values in which parents attempt to exercise control through finances.

A parent may, for example, be instrumental in impeding a relationship and may do everything possible to pull a couple apart. Financial support may be withdrawn.

On the other hand, a parent may be a source of needed backing. Money may appear surprisingly from one's own parents or from the parents of the partner in the relationship.

This is, to some extent, a card of expressed needs, of seeking out security and warmth, and of a loving and supportive material environment. The *Seven of Cups* means transition; the goal is ultimately attained, but the overcoming of obstacles requires effort, hardship and, not infrequently, sacrifice.

EIGHT OF CUPS

Change

The *Eight of Cups* is a card of changeability and of romantic flitting from one idea to another. Feeling and intuition are more important than thinking. Amusing pastimes are pursued, most often those which captivate only briefly. Dancing and music are, of course, favorites. And although there may be an intellectual grasp of a great many subjects, understanding is always superficial. There is little real mastery in any area.

The card may show an immature personality, one who is unable to make permanent commitments. On the other hand, affiliation with partners, societies, associations, and companies is indicated, and although such relationships may be short-lived, they tend to be profitable. The card suggests a variety of superficial pursuits, but many of these projects are likely to succeed.

The best return may be through occupations connected with land deals, such as real estate sales or development. There is also a possibility of financial support from the mother or from some understanding person on her side of the family.

NINE OF CUPS

Vascillation

This is a free flow of ideas, of emotions, of thoughts, of inner pictures and of experiences. One's thoughts and behavior may be directed from outside, or they may be controlled by the feelings of others — in which case there may be terrible uncertainty, an inability to focus clearly, and a sense of purposelessness in one's life. Yet if the free flow is one of consciousness purposely evoked and perfectly controlled, it is quite a different matter.

Many meanings of *Nine of Cups* are apparently negative. Yet this can be an extremely powerful card, depending upon surrounding influences. The card may describe a mystical and intentional diminishing of focus on the personality, i.e., on the self in incarnation. It may describe a purposeful loosening of the the bonds of perceived "reality," and an increasing ability to consciously interact with the materials of the unconscious.

Symbolically, the reference is to phases of the Moon and to water, both of which decribe the Mother. And, in fact, at its most profound level — and in Jungian terms — this card describes the process by which the Mother teaches the son to meditate effectively.

TEN OF CUPS

Pain and Sorrow

By any standard this is the worst, the most devastating card in the deck, one which — in astrological symbolism — refers to Saturn in Cancer. It means the ultimate anti-thesis, Earth plunged into the uncertainty of Water. In Jungian terms, this may be described as the destruction of the waking consciousness's structure of "reality," by immersion in the collective unconscious. There is a total destruction without appeal.

The card can mean death, but it does not refer to death as a transition as does the trump card of that title. The death here is absolute and does not flow into something else. It is the total end of a cycle of things as previously known.

The world of the individual may be turned upside down. There may be downfall, loss of profession, divorce, banishment, loss of wealth, loss of health, loss of love.

The implications are so overwhelming that one can only respond philosophically, and with resignation. It may be suggested that each person must suffer at the hands of fate. The tradition of the Western mystery schools states, in fact, that we are the architect of our every experience. We get what we earn, what we need and, ultimately, what we choose unconsciously.

KING OF SWORDS

The Romantic Father

This is a strong-willed and active person who is basically a romantic. On the surface he may appear aggressive, gregarious, and amused by company. Yet at base he seeks solitude and harmony. He usually appears calm and reasonable, but can be very volatile. His temper may flare out of control, but anger is quickly expended. He forgives and forgets very quickly.

He loves change and new ideas, bores easily, and enjoys things which others may find eccentric and bizarre. He tends to surround himself with odd, and often very creative, characters to the occasional dismay of his family and long-term friends.

The *King of Wands* is independent in all that he does, and would rather hold court than listen to the ideas of others. He is a loner; he often acts without concern for the reactions of others and is willing to take an unpopular stand.

His personality is not well-suited to marriage. A partner may find him a constant source of surprises — good and bad — but he may also be aloof, withdrawn, and moody.

At his best he is charming, witty, intelligent, and entertaining. At his worst he can be cruel, thoughtless, even ruthless in his dealings with others.

QUEEN OF SWORDS

The Diplomatic Mother

The *Queen of Swords* is a delightful woman of exceptional social skills. She is at once perceptive, sensitive, and flexible — never wishing to offend, always willing to listen and to compromise. She will, occasionally, give in to bad ideas to avoid conflict — which she finds extremely unpleasant.

This woman is a consummate diplomat who avoids confrontation unless she feels that she has been wronged, in which case those who know her only casually may find the force of her response astonishing. But her closest friends appreciate that her inner feelings and thoughts are very different from what she projects.

Her life is drawn in two somewhat contradictory directions: Family and home are all-important to her; she draws strength from her family. Yet her interpersonal abilities bring her to the forefront of career and social situations, and she finds herself balancing delicately between the two worlds.

On the negative side, she is actually very self-centered and has little interest in either social causes or the rights of others. She can be both deceitful and disingenuous, and always chooses sides and points of view which will bring her the greatest personal advantage in a given situation.

PRINCE OF SWORDS

The Idealist Son

Here is a graceful, charming, and romantic young man, an idealist who may rely too much on others. He loves to love, and seeks refuge from a coarse world in his inner mind and in story book fantasies. He may be an artist or a poet, and is a delightful friend and companion, one who is able to find interest and beauty where others may not see it.

On the other hand, because he seeks the ideal, perfection in all things, he is very disappointed and hurt by those who cannot measure up. He is kind, gentle, and extremely intelligent, yet he can be gullible and easily reached through his emotions.

He feels very deeply and may experience (or himself cause) some very painful relationships. He may, from time to time, completely withdraw from society and may even become seriously emotionally ill.

He runs from conflict and from confrontation — is a pacifist at heart. Because so much of what he does is a response to others, his contributions cannot be separated from the situations in which he may find himself, and from the people with whom he associates.

PRINCESS OF SWORDS

The Controlling Daughter

The Controlling Daughter is an orderly young woman who keeps her feelings under firm control, and who takes very few chances in interpersonal relationships. She is cautious, prudent, and sometimes selfish, but is generally well-liked and successful in whatever she attempts.

She is a shrewd manager who gets exactly what she wants and for whom the end justifies the means. She seeks power, and is not above dealings which may be unethical or even illegal. She is relatively unconcerned about other people, but she manipulates so well that this is not immediately obvious.

Although this Princess is quite independent, she is admired by colleagues in a business or profession – who consider her to be a team player. But, in fact, her loyalties are available to the highest bidder. She would be an ideal executive for a large corporation, where her political and managerial skills would guarantee rapid advance.

Some may complain that she projects arrogance, even toughness, but this is protective. She is a vulnerable and sensitive young woman who cannot afford to allow a potential adversary to know what she is thinking.

ACE OF SWORDS

Conflict of Ideas

This is a power struggle; this is a card of ideological conflict, of battle over principle and over points of view where the strongest (not necessarily the best) advocate is the victor. Great force comes into play and exposes secrets which may be shocking. The real truth comes out in the midst of the fight, and someone may be seriously hurt — emotionally, physically, and perhaps financially. The struggle can be very violent, very direct, and very open. There is no subtlety of conflict such as that found in the *Ace of Cups*.

Yet something positive always emerges as mind-sets are played one against the other. A whole new idea or sets of principles may result. Preconceived notions and intellectual position may be overturned; outworn ideas may be discarded. This may happen on a small scale between individuals, either at home or at work, or it may happen between great nations.

The *Ace of Swords* represents the very basis of thought — the root of thought itself. Swords are the suit of the Son, and what we call "thought" is the joint product of Mother-Female-Unconscious and Father-Male-Creative Spirit.

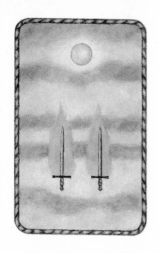

TWO OF SWORDS

Opposition and Loss

The *Two of Swords* means rivalry, opposition, and criticism. There is no possibility of resolution to a problem; an end is reached. A friendship may be destroyed, or a marriage ended either in divorce or in the death of the spouse.

In a work situation this may mean the end of a partnership, or of some important business relationship. A position may be lost to someone else, or a person may be discharged. The card can also mean financial loss caused by ill-considered speculation, in which case it also refers to the breach of a relationship with persons or organizations involved, such as a stockbroker or a bank.

Collapse, negative verdict, or loss, is the inevitable result of impulsive action, of a passionate urge somehow misapplied and for which the individual must accept responsibility. Yet this same urge toward change, the same "opposition" and loss of what has been secure, is very positive when applied to painting, to literature, to music, or to any of the arts, and the result is quite favorable. In that regard, the card represents increased imagination and intuition.

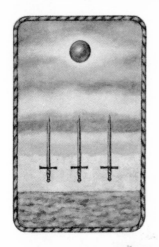

THREE OF SWORDS

Idealism

There is here an idealistic, if not completely unrealistic, approach to society and to individual relationships. The card suggests a revolt against institutional structures, although not necessarily a purposeful attempt to overthrow or to change structure. It means, rather, an unwillingness to go along with planned programs, and to seek new and untried paths.

This is a card of pioneering and of creative imagination which spells success in almost any artistic endeavor if a person is sufficiently disciplined to "ground" new ideas. Emotions are very important and may not always be backed up by practical instincts. When that is the case, there may be a lack of personal focus and a difficulty in making decisions which can spell trouble in business or in financial situations. Moreover, one may be self-deceiving, believing a relationship to be something that it is not. Sexual attraction can be especially important, and may be the basis of a brief infatuation.

In a serious and understanding friendship, love, or marriage such "idealism" will generally be positive, and means starting things out on the right foot.

FOUR OF SWORDS

Imagination

The energies represented by this card are among the most positive of the deck. Indeed, imagination is the key to human progress; creative vision is that which carries civilization forward in the arts, in science, in politics, and in every aspect of society.

Here the mind touches upon an inner "something" which can enervate and inspire, a condition which makes the person very attractive to others, who are delighted with the projection of artistic and poetic thoughts. So this is a card of good feelings, of caring and of friendship. It also relates to mysticism and to religious feelings because the source of one's imagination remains a secret to others. Under very inauspicious conditions, there may be secret treachery or a rather negative fluidity of ideas producing an inability to focus.

At its most profound, the *Four of Swords* stands for a magical journey into unconscious possibility, and the bringing back of ideas and images which affect daily life in some way. But, as with every card of, there can also be a very basic and mundane interpretation. The could mean, quite simply, a good and safe journey.

FIVE OF SWORDS

Rash Decision

The *Five of Swords* shows unconsidered action and rapid choice. It means a decision, reached with little or no hesitation, which may lead to good or to bad results depending entirely upon the circumstances. Feeling is more important than thought and an action may be in frustration when the "right" decision is unclear. One may act on intuition, or on the vague suspicion that a course is appropriate.

There may also be a powerful sexual involvement, a very intense love, or perhaps a hasty marriage. The significant consideration here is that a binding commitment is made very rapidly. This could mean an expensive purchase made on whim, and really beyond one's means to afford.

An important business commitment, such as a partnership could be hurriedly formed, or a contract could be hastily drawn up and signed. The result may be very positive if those involved are cooperative and understanding.

But the rash decision may represent a disastrous choice. Emotions may clash, rivalry may emerge. Under very

100

negative conditions this could mean broken promises or contracts, or it could mean the death of a partner or of a friend.

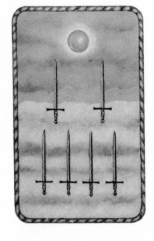

SIX OF SWORDS

Justice

This is a highly intellectual card which means justice, harmony, and laws upheld with sensitivity. It is a card of balance and of compromise. And as the *Six of Swords* refers to the reconciliation of opposites, it may suggest the result of some very astute diplomacy applied to a family or to a business situation.

Great compassion and wisdom are involved in a decision in which the judge is positive and self-assured. This may actually be a lawsuit or other legal action, in which case, and assuming good circumstances, it is likely to be resolved with considerable fairness. Under very bad conditions there may be indecision or an inability to reach a just conclusion — the obverse potential of the card.

As "Justice," this card means completed decision and resolve, rather than the process by which a decision takes place. It can mean justice applied as in a court, or in any situation where the individual is assessed. Frequently, however, it refers to each person's own decisions and reconciliation of conflicting actions, ideas, and emotional urges.

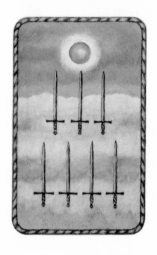

SEVEN OF SWORDS

Love

The *Seven of Swords* means almost perfect happiness, and although every card has negative potential, that is only possible here under the most dire of circumstances.

This is the essence of love and of marriage, a union which is virtually ideal, with partners who beautifully complement each other and who share completely at all levels. The card can also mean intense and understanding friendship where two people bring great gifts to each others lives.

Popularity and sociability are highlighted with warm gatherings of family and friends and a sense of fulfillment in all that one does. Two individuals are seen by others as compassionate, and as living in a state of almost mystical harmony.

All needs are met, emotional, intellectual, and physical. Money is assured, possibly through marriage, or perhaps through a friend or partner. In business this can mean a special kind of sharing, between one or more people, which leads to a very great degree of success.

In the event of truly disastrous circumstances, the positive qualities — the love, the harmony, and the happiness — remain, althrough they are somewhat diminished.

EIGHT OF SWORDS

Intellectual Skill

All of the qualities making for accomplished writing and scholarship are represented here — not merely thought, but also creative inspiration. For a novelist this may mean a plot which emerges effortlessly; for a research scholar this may mean a unique and insightful overview of materials; for a teacher this may mean extraordinary command of a subject and the ability to communicate it with clarity and flair.

There is a certain poetry — a refined pleasure in dealing with ideas, and the ability to express those ideas in words

— which bring the ideas to life for others. Communication is important, and a person may earn considerable money through publications which gain wide popularity. The aspects here almost insure that works will be well received.

Manipulation of business concepts and dealings is also highly favored by such clear-sighted and inventive approaches. One is likely to receive strong support from a partner or from colleagues, and may, in a large company, move quickly upward.

The card is almost always positive but, under very unfavorable circumstances, there may be vascillation, delay, and an inability to choose a clear course of action.

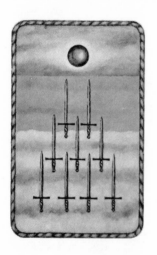

NINE OF SWORDS

Sharing

The *Nine of Swords* means working with others. It means understanding and good-natured cooperation. In a marriage or in a very close friendship the day-to-day activities and responsibilities are comfortably shared, with each person more or less anticipating the needs of the other. The same holds true for a business situation in which the partners mesh well. Great generosity is indicated, but it cannot be considered charitable because there is equal give and take. Refinement and charm are evident in the relationship.

This is an active ongoing process which is courteous and pleasant. Giving is done with affection. On the other hand, results are not suggested (as they are in the *Ten*). In business, for example, the fact that two partners work well together and create a warm environment may be wonderful, but it does not insure profit.

If something goes wrong it is likely to be worked out amicably. Problems are solved easily because there is so much mutual respect and admiration. The worst that is likely to happen, under very adverse conditions, is that one person becomes selfish, and the balance is somewhat thrown off.

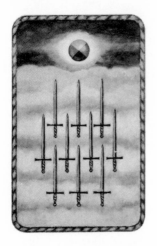

TEN OF SWORDS

Gain Through Partnership

This is success resulting from people working smoothly together — either in partnership or in association of some sort. It is likely that two partners are very different, in age, in temperament, or in social position, yet they complement each other perfectly — one contributing exactly what the other lacks. Theirs is a mutual goal of wealth and position which is the sure result of their sharing of responsibilities.

The partnership seems charmed as obstacles melt away and money is earned. These uniquely compatible partners create an ideally well-functioning company which produces enviable profits. There is hard work and long hours, but the return on the investment is considerable.

In terms of home and family, a marriage is productive, prosperous, and free of problems. The environment may be quite refined and elegant, radiating a sense of harmony.

Under negative conditions, something may go wrong — partners may begin to disagree and to challenge each other's decisions. There may be disloyalty, bad feelings, and serious misunderstandings which cause profits to diminish.

KING OF PENTACLES

The Responsible Father

This King is an extremely independent and assertive man, one who is strong and uncompromising, and who holds prominence and enormous responsibility. He may be a powerful executive of a large business. He is always willing to listen, yet he is egocentric and demanding, always believing that whatever he decides is right.

His keenly critical intellect is applied to material projects; he is uninterested in religion, in philosophy, or in the arts. On the other hand, he judges and hires creative people astutely when he sees that they may help bring some material advantage.

He is impatient and restless to get things done, a tireless worker who makes very strict demands on those around him. There are few who understand him, and on whom he feels he can depend absolutely, but he rewards loyalty.

He lacks romance, is rather cold blooded, and tends to ruffle feathers as he asks of others the same dedication that he demands from himself. He is a man of considerable integrity, but when cornered, or in a bad situation, he may act with ruthlessness, a disregard for others, and even cruelty.

QUEEN OF PENTACLES

The Secretive Mother

The woman in this card is economical to an extreme. She is cautious about the way she handles money — never wanting to put out more than is absolutely necessary, and always wanting to get the most value for the least cost.

She is even more reserved in her interpersonal relationships, being wary about letting people into her private world. A selfish person, she seeks business success and feels that the goal of wealth and power justifies the means.

The great secretiveness about her personal life and about her profession — the fact that she never wants people to know exactly what she is thinking or feeling — stems partly from a desire never to reliquish control. It also reflects a sense of insecurity so deeply-ingrained that some might consider her to suffer from borderline paranoia.

At her best she may be an extremely astute businesswoman, a very good mother and provider who may, herself, have come from a family with considerable financial resources. At her worst she can be untrusting, and the source of some very devious plots and plans which generate bad feelings among her friends and coworkers.

PRINCE OF PENTACLES

The Self-Assured Son

This is a thoughtful and self-assured young man who is certain that he is right, and who does not easily listen to the ideas of others. But, whatever goal he may pursue, he does so persistently and achieves success — largely through the force of his personality. This is true especially when he can bring himself to compromise.

He is popular and well-liked — a good companion whose outgoing qualities and playful eccentricities are greatly admired. He can be a gentle and caring partner in a relationship, despite a tendency to be detached and impatient.

His frequent and usually correct intuitions lead him to an interest in metaphysics and to the occult although he has an inner conflict about what to believe. This may be attributed to early religious training, but it is more the result of a natural pragmatism which makes him most comfortable with the cause and effect relationships of science.

Under negative or very stressful conditions he can be arrogant and demanding, and tends to alienate those around him. He is unlikely to admit his own fault, but insists that others are responsible for whatever problems may occur.

PRINCESS OF PENTACLES

The Isolated Daughter

Shown here is a very isolated and introspective young woman. She is steady, ambitious, thorough — one who is basically quite competent at her work, yet she is a "loner." She is self-controlled, tactful, and reserved, but she is also very selfish in attaining her own goals.

In a position of responsibility she may offend people by harsh demands and by showing little interest in the ideas or feelings of subordinates. She knows that she is not well-liked, but does not consider herself at fault.

She tends to judge everything in polar terms, has little tolerance for ambiguity, wants situations to be clearly-defined, and is not particularly subtle. She finds the arts quite boring and, with the possible exception of watching sports events, has few outside interests. She spends long hours buried in work, which allows her to avoid the personal interaction of a normal social life.

She has few friends, and is often depressed and lonely. But she hides her vulnerabilities well. Most perceive her as unaffectionate and unfeeling. The problem, however, is that she is afraid of closeness and somehow never learned the social skills of communicating personal feelings.

ACE OF PENTACLES

Security Destroyed

This is a revolution in the material world, a devastating and painful experience in which secure and dependable structures are utterly destroyed and cleared away. In the most basic of terms, this could mean urban renewal – old city buildings demolished so that new ones can be contructed in their place. Or this could mean a revolution which brings down one government with the intention of substituting another.

Here is a traumatic event, and a subsequent void of uncertainty about what may come next. The dust has not settled; nothing is clear or certain.

In business, this could mean total ruin and bankruptcy, or the collapse of a financial institution and the resulting fear and panic. In personal terms, a marriage may collapse, a family may disintegrate, a home may be destroyed.

Philosophically, *The Ace of Pentacles* represents the basis of all substance and the principle that matter is self-renewing. This is shown graphically in the *uroboros*, the snake which holds its tail in its mouth. The practical message if that in our lives voids are only apparent; insecurity is a transient and necessarily cyclic condition.

TWO OF PENTACLES

Reorganization

The *Two of Pentacles* represents a highly original and organized restructuring, a change which is thoughtfully and intelligently administered. Generally, this reorganization happens from within, and is the product of ambition and of individual genius.

Accepted authority is challenged; outworn structures are reshaped and replaced. This is likely to happen very swiftly. But it may be the result of long effort and great perseverance on the part of one person, one leader of great vision.

The energies are very favorable to those in public occupations and in positions of authority — to all who need to act with creativity and with certainty. A dynamically inventive person brings about fundamental and positive changes and receives considerable credit.

This is a very strong card which describes change without values implied. What emerges is not necessarily better — it is simply different from what it replaced. Moreover, the challenge to structure may be abrasive and, in unfavorable conditions, may produce negative feelings, public criticism, and censure from superiors.

THREE OF PENTACLES

Response to Conflict

The conflicts involved are of changing social structure in a home or in a work situation. This may be the result of trouble through the family early in life, especially through the father. There may be an eccentric, or very ambivalent, attitude and response to conflict with authority figures generally. The confrontation is a dark, inner, one. And the "response" may be very unclear.

Psychologically this is a particularly interesting card in that it often suggests repressed materials of childhood, feelings about authority figures nurtured early, to which one unconsciously responds as an adult. This may mean expressing repressed hostility toward an authoritarian father figure by, for example, over-reacting to the demands of a strong employer. At other levels, the card suggests an increase in money and finances. It also heralds success in art, in music, or in occupations related to philosophy and religion — all of which tend to delve deeply into unconscious materials, and to "bring them down" into a world of structure.

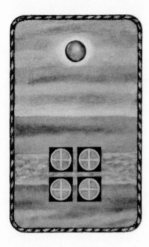

FOUR OF PENTACLES

Wealth

A great deal of money is involved, possibly inherited, and it is handled with care, frugality, and with an understanding of its value. This card does not suggest the sudden appearance of wealth, rather it describes the condition and responsibilities of vast personal resources, something of the point of view which has often been described as "old money."

There is a very serious, humorless, approach to resources. But wealth is not seen as an end in itself; what matters is the process of dealing with money, as does the maintenance of a certain life-style.

Administration is carried out with enthusiasm and with great skill. The person wins popularity and esteem from subordinates, and find superiors always willing to assist.

Success in an executive career, or in anything involving management of large amounts of money, and of large numbers of people, is assured. Everything seems to work perfectly, achievement and prosperity flow in.

Apart from wealth *per se*, the *Four of Pentacles* (interpreted as Jupiter in Capricorn) may suggest an unorthodox approach to religion.

114

FIVE OF PENTACLES

Responsible Authority

The person in authority represented here is quite ambitious, and has earned a position of prominence through hard work and through willingness to accept significant responsibilities. The pursuit of money and of material comforts is important; wealth inherited from family may have initially made possible an executive position.

Duties are taken seriously and are performed in a disciplined and thoughtful way. Good results appear: a business is smooth-running and profitable, a family is comfortable and well-provided.

But a tendency toward impatience and irritability may bring conflict with co-workers and, especially, with superiors. Assertive behavior causes criticism, and not infrequently jealousy.

At home there is the possibility of friction with a parent or with brothers and sisters. Disagreements and misunderstandings are usually minor, but those not smoothed out quickly tend to build resentments which become serious and result in irreconcilable separations, discharge from employment, divorce, separation, and even death.

SIX OF PENTACLES

Gain of Wealth and Power Through Hard Work

The *Six of Pentacles* stands for unswerving self-discipline, for long and hard work which yields impressive results, often against very substantial odds or in opposition to many who say that something cannot be done. A person is driven toward one ambitious goal, and has the strength of character never to be moved from the course toward that goal.

The road can be very solitary and requiring of great patience and perseverance. There are some very dark periods of uncertainty and depression before the goal is attained. But self-assurance and other aggressive personality qualities guarantee eventual success.

Here is an extravert who reaches out toward others easily, yet whose behavior is under absolute control. Clarity in communication is essential. Time is money. A well-organized procedure is established and followed.

One's efforts may lead to the pinnacle of achievement, and others may be inspired by example. Yet this successful person may be perceived by fellow-workers as humorless and cold, as overly strict, as one who is "all work and no play" and who appears to place money, power, and personal success ahead of people and their feelings.

116

SEVEN OF PENTACLES

Gain Through Commerce

This is a powerful card of almost certain financial reward through business, investments, stocks or banking. A responsible position is indicated. The favor of superiors is earned, but rarely that of co-workers — who consider the person aloof and unfriendly, cold and calculating.

What is shown here is very different from the *Six of Pentacles*. As opposed to "hard work," the *Seven* may mean genius at business management, manipulation, guile, and financial gamesmanship which has little to do with the amount of time or effort expended. A fortune may be made in a five minute phone call to a stock broker.

Generally the pursuit of money and rewards is done to the exclusion of all else; friends and family are secondary, co-workers are merely pawns to be used as necessary. It is possible that a marriage may be delayed, or a friendship destroyed because of the attention devoted to business.

On a somewhat negative note: there may be a deep inner struggle between ambition at work and the emotional demands of family and friends. Or business may be a convenient emotional escape from personal responsibilities.

EIGHT OF PENTACLES

Manipulation and Secrets

Without question this is one of the most intriguing and mysterious cards of the Tarot. It means the essence of subtlety and diplomacy applied to some specific end. Great intelligence and seriousness is involved in a very detailed presentation. A plan appears accurate and complete, but is really a cover for secret ideas and intentions. The totality is never shown openly: events are surreptitiously arranged; people are discreetly manipulated without their knowledge.

Caution and critical attention to detail is essential. The agenda is hidden, but what emerges is of profound significance. This could mean academic honors, very serious news, the offer of an important position, or something agreed upon in private consideration and negotiation.

It cannot be said, generally, that the *Eight of Pentacles* represents either a good or a bad situation. It is, rather, a condition of *sub rosa* activity, the results of which depend on what has gone before and the people involved. If surrounding influences are positive, secret work will yield results of excellence and strength. With negative conditions, this card may suggest the presence of dishonesty, lies, or a vicious plot.

118

NINE OF PENTACLES

Selfishness

This is a card of egocentric control in which one who is totally unconcerned about the feelings of others uses a cautious and calculating exercise of will for personal gain. It is a card of attitude, of perspective, which may be either good or bad, depending upon circumstances. The focus is quite basic; everything revolves around a person's getting what they want, materially and emotionally.

At best, a person may rightly have earned, and be deserving of attention — such as a great actor who has come to expect deference. At worst, this selfish point of view may be be very negative, even destructive. A person may be ruthless, taking the attitude that any means, no matter how brutal, justifies the end reward. This extreme exemplifies the antisocial personality — for whom there is no right or wrong, only self-gratification and the flaunting of social regulations and conventions by which others must abide.

Whatever the case, the individual is the center of attention. This could mean favors and popularity, or it could mean a notorious scandal bringing about personal attacks and loss of reputation.

TEN OF PENTACLES

Isolated Power

The *Ten of Pentacles* shows a strong individual who is uniquely alone in the exercise of tremendous power and control in social, in business, in political, or in other situations. Ambitions and desires are very structured; nothing is more important than gaining money and position. And there is a studied directness, a certain roughness and arrogance, which others may find disarming.

Although this person may be envied, the position is a very isolated one where ideas, feelings and, most of all, personal problems cannot be shared. In fact, apparent strength may hide personal insecurities and, not infrequently, a sense of loneliness and of unfulfilled desire for personal interaction.

Life at a pinnacle may be exciting, or it may be sad. Under the most adverse conditions this card can refer to personal downfall — a devastating loss of money and of profession. Usually, however, the card represents a person isolated by success — by the very fact of winning (and maintaining) the power and wealth which has been aggressively sought.

A 34 Week Course of Studies
Using the Jungian Tarot Cards
for the Development
of Self-Understanding

Self-exploration with the Jungian Tarot involves the creation of a sort of fantasy play, a dialog with oneself which is totally honest. You will deal initially with Mother and Father, and then with their projected attributes, Son and Daughter. Finally you will consider the behavioral patterns and situations represented by the remaining cards. It should be noted here that meditation with *The Fool* is assigned only after considerable experience in active imagination has been gained with the other cards of the Major Arcana.

BEFORE BEGINNING: Resolve to initially pursue a disciplined twenty-two week course of meditation with the Major Arcana, working with a given card two times a week for at least fifteen minutes — and for no longer than thirty minutes. Determine that nothing will deter you from this exercise.

Find a place which is quiet and where there is little chance of being interrupted. Meditations should be done soon after arising in the morning, and on an empty stomach.

SELF-DISCOVERY THROUGH THE MAJOR ARCANA (22 WEEKS)

STEP ONE: Select the card of *The Empress*.

STEP TWO: Sit quietly in a chair either holding the card, or with it propped up. After a few moments of intense concentration on the image, close your eyes and attempt to "see" the figure in an inner landscape. For some this is easy, for others it is very difficult, but creative visualization is a skill which improves with practice. Those who find it difficult to "see" initially should not strain, but should attempt to use other senses, such as touch — reaching out to feel a rock, or the branch of a tree. Or some may easily smell or hear. Follow the sense which is the easiest and sight will take care of itself.

STEP THREE: Ask some question of the inner figure, such as "who are you?" The Empress (as a matter of what some would describe as "talking to oneself,") may say "I am mother," or "I love you," or "why don't you leave me alone," or something utterly irrational such as "goldfish." (The more irrational these conversations, the closer they are coming to the buried contents of our personal unconscious).

STEP FOUR: Allow the conversation to develop. In any of the 78 cards, you may find yourself in a variety of landscapes or interiors with the figure which may lead you in some way, and which may be shape-shifting. Your mind may wander a great deal in the beginning (control will be easier after some practice) and should be brought back to the figure of The Empress or to whatever figure may evolve.

STEP FIVE: End the exercise by standing, by stretching, and then by stamping a foot on the ground. This tends to forcefully separate the dream-world from waking reality, and to help avoid dissociation — a very common effect of such meditative exercises. If an uncomfortable sense of detachment does occur, eating something will usually clear it up.

STEP SIX: In a diary, write down everything that you can recall of your interaction with "Mother."

This is the basic technique, to be applied to one card a week in the following sequence and exploring some of the following ideas with each card figure:

Week 1. **Empress**: Inner relationship with your own Mother.

Week 2. **Emperor**: Inner relationship with your own Father.

Week 3. **Magician**: The role of Son; ways in which the Son remains part of the Father; the idea of male; male aspect of yourself; Son = Daughter.

Week 4. **High Priestess**: The role of Daughter; ways in which the Daughter remains part of the Mother; the idea of female, female aspect of yourself; Daughter = Son.

Week 5. **Hierophant**: The Father who creates rules; your attitudes toward regulation and the parent who states them.

Week 6. **Lover**: The Son who gathers life experience and who applies the lessons of the Mother and of the Father.

Week 7. **Chariot**: The Father whose presence you somehow always feel — (and cannot escape).

Week 8. **Strength**: The Daughter who gathers life experience and who applies the lessons of the Mother and of the Father.

Week 9. **Wheel of Fortune**: The Mother who determines the experience of the Son or of the Daughter.

Week 10. **Tower**: The Father who protects and provides.

Week 11. **Justice:** The Mother who punishes and rewards.

Week 12. **Death:** The Mother as passageway — physically at birth, and symbolically at the gateway of death; thoughts about your own mortality.

Week 13. **Temperance:** The Daughter as mediator; the urge to resolve extremes as a quality in each person.

Week 14. **Devil:** The Dark Son; boldly facing our negative qualities — ourselves at the worst; archetype of shadow.

Week 15. **Hanged Man**: The Son who turns from the world; your conscious thought which seeks to immerse itself in a greater consciousness; considering the relationship of your individual thought world to those of others.

Week 16. **Star**: The Virgin Daughter; adolescence; the first steps toward independence from the parents.

Week 17. **The Hermit**: The Grandfather who is the Wise Teacher; the passage of life from Grandfather to Father to Son.

Week 18. **The Moon**: The Deadly Mother; Grandmother as witch; the Mother who threatens the Son with death, who subjects him to brutal trials; our own Mother's hostility sometimes toward us (a fleeting death wish toward one's own children is very common).

Week 19. **The Sun**: The Child; reconciliation of the masculine and feminine aspects; return to a state of innocence where one may begin in a new way.

Week 20. **Judgment**: The Son who judges, who evaluates; an inner figure which observes and evaluates your progress at all levels.

124

Week 21. **The World:** The Daughter who hides her face; a feminine figure which creates the mask "Persona" by which she is known; concealed thoughts and feelings.

Week 22. **The Fool:** The embodiment of Spirit; the abstract source of dualities — of male and female; where we come from and where we are going; the nature of life.

Psychological Principles

In using the card of *The Empress* as doorway into a self-created dream vision, our first conversation is, by definition, with a personal concept of mother derived from interaction with our own mother figure. *The Emperor* is, of course, the father figure. To deal with either of them may require that we face, head-on, some painfully unresolved issues about our relationship to mother or to father.

It may be discovered that there are some deeply repressed and unpleasant feelings. There may also be repressed good feelings, such as those which might remind us of the loss of a parent with whom we had wonderfully pleasant experiences.

We may say to *The Empress* or to *The Emperor* (under whatever guise they appear) in an absolutely unguarded way: "I need you so much," or "Please stand by me," or "I despise you," or even "You never loved me." Moreover, feelings such as sexual desire toward the parent, or a serious desire to do physical violence (the sex and violence urges are closely related) are not uncommon, and are even normal. What emerges from these inner contacts is a spectrum of thoughts and of behavior patterns which is quite natural to us as human animals, but which our culture teaches us to repress.

In fact, much of our initial work of self-discovery through the cards is an admission, to ourselves, of who we really are and of what our relationship to family, friends, co-workers, etc., may be. The operative principle is that, again using *The Empress* as an example, we must have totally resolved our relationship with our own mother, before we can even begin to approach the profound Mother Archetype of the collective unconscious.

The more one experiments with the cards, and the more repressed materials are encountered and overcome with understanding, the deeper the meditations become, and the more the universal aspects of the figures as archetypes are perceived. These are the essential mechanics of the developing process which Jung called "individuation," and which tradition has called "enlightenment."

One additional point should be made about these imaginary conversations. The dream world in our minds must be thought of as animistic, where there is life and intelligence in everything. Some surprising results will be achieved by addressing questions to rocks and trees and to other inanimate objects. A tree can turn into a child; flowers may grow in rocks; a lake may catch fire. The rules of "reality" do not apply and we may feel ourselves cast into the magic kingdom of the brothers Grimm and Hans Christian Andersen.

This is true whether one is dealing with the cards of the Major or of the Minor Arcana.

PERSONALITY-ANALYSIS THROUGH THE COURT CARDS (4 WEEKS)

The Technique

The course of meditation with the 16 Court Cards increases from two to four days in each week. *Each day you should first read the description of the personality.* Otherwise, the methodology is almost identical to that used with the Major Arcana, and begins as you address questions to a given figure.

Through the Court Cards you will consider your interaction with others. In this regard, professional therapists may find the Court Card "families" especially useful as projective devices, or for the stimulation of discussion.

Your imaginary conversation with the Kings, Queens, Princes, and Princesses, as different types of personalities, will have a remarkable effect on your understanding and control of interpersonal relationships. You will come to understand the ways in which you deal with different types of people in a variety of contexts — home, work, school, etc.

In conversing with an imaginary individual, try to define the ways in which you relate to someone with a given personality. Do you give in to someone more aggressive, or are you always ready to argue? When faced with a charming and engaging person, do you feel a sense of envy, or do you perhaps feel a sense of competition? What type of person attracts you? What type of person repels you? And in either case, is your behavior controlled?

The second, and perhaps most important, thing for you to determine is the reason that you react to different personalities as you do. You may be amazed what you can learn about yourself by simply asking these imaginary persons why they think you react to them as you do and, equally important — what they think of you.

What you may find most surprising about this method is that although we all tend to endow our "antagonist personalities" with largely negative qualities, it is, in these exercises, almost impossible to avoid considering the other person's point of view. Court cards are empathy-producing.

Each person will begin an inner conversation differently. One might say to the *King of Wands*: "Why do you think I depend on you so much?"

Another might ask: "Why do you keep pushing me around?"

And yet another might say: "Don't you think we're a lot alike?"

Week 1. **King of Wands**: An aggressive man.
Queen of Wands: A stylish woman.
Prince of Wands: An affectionate young man.
Princess of Wands: A clever young woman.

Week 2. **King of Cups**: A very intelligent man.
Queen of Cups: An emotional woman.
Prince of Cups: A charming young man.
Princess of Cups: An ambitious young woman.

Week 3. **King of Swords**: A romantic man.
Queen of Swords: A diplomatic woman.
Prince of Swords: An idealistic young man.
Princess of Swords: A controlling young woman.

Week 4. **King of Pentacles**: A responsible man.
Queen of Pentacles: A secretive woman.
Prince of Pentacles: A self-assured young man.
Princess of Pentacles: An isolated young woman.

SITUATIONAL-ANALYSIS THROUGH THE MINOR CARDS (8 WEEKS)

Technique

The Minor Cards require a unique approach as they represent a review (or preview) of our decisions and behavior. In this very advanced and difficult course of exercises, which requires five days of each week, you will read the card description and then immerse yourself in the situation described for a card meditating on the implications of those qualities and experiences by acting them out with imaginary players on an imaginary stage of your own design. The technique of using the card requires the level of experience gained by working with the Major Arcana and the Court cards.

It will be discovered that, although at first glance these forty cards appear all too similar and unremarkable, concentration on each image evokes an unexplainably different feeling. There is here, quite literally, "much more than meets the eye." And in fact some very knowledgeable specialists in Tarot have, over the years, suggested that the Minor Cards are actually of far greater importance than are either the Major Arcana or the Court cards insofar as they suggest *pure number* under different influences.

The least that can be promised with certainty is that the excercise of creative imagination with these simple and largely amorphous stimuli will, if seriously pursued, lead to some remarkable insights.

In proceeding, you may choose to create an experience as if to ask: "In such a case, how would I respond and what would happen?" Or you may choose to "replay" some event in which you might now act differently than you did originally, asking the participants about their feelings toward you and toward the situation. All in all, the procedure is not unlike that of theatrical studies, where actors learn to improvise.

As an experience is being recalled, or created, you will focus on the design and begin to "read into" it people, or buildings, or whatever may relate to the experience in question. For example, a face may begin to emerge from the water, or a figure may be seen darting from behind one of the Fire Wands. You should stare at the card for a few minutes and let these images emerge, and until the card's design seems to dissolve. Then close your eyes.

The principle here is that you imagine yourself to be the object of the quality or behavior represented by the card. A few examples may be considered:

Six of Wands, Impulsive Leadership. Imagine yourself subject to a person who acts without thinking. How do you respond? Do you try to reason with the person and work with the problem, or do you become angry and leave? Imagine a conversation with such a person.

Five of Cups, Troubles. Everyone can recall a very difficult situation of perhaps loss of job, divorce, financial difficulties. Recreate such a situation involving at least one other person, and try to determine how you handled it and whether you assigned blame. Were you afraid? Did your emotions get in the way of clear action? In retrospect, would you now behave differently? If so, play the experience out as you might now respond to it.

Three of Wands, Fantasy. How do you deal with the fantasies of others? Do you deprecate them? Do you share them? Do you view fantasy as positive or negative? As an interesting exercise you might first imagine a conversation with an artist or creative writer, and then create a mind-play with one who uses fantasy to escape into a dream world.

130

The process may sound complicated, but we do exactly the same thing when we stare out the window of a train and daydream. The difference here is that we choose our topic consciously. Through the card a play begins to unfold.

The Minor Cards help to develop problem-solving abilities by focusing concentration on a specific life experience and the appropriate actions of the individual in response to that experience.

The mechanics of this exercise are similar to those of work with the Court cards. First you will attempt to define the way you behave when faced with a certain situation, and then you will look for the reasons for your response. Follow this schedule of meditations on the cards:

Week 1. **Ace** through **Five of Wands**
Week 2. **Six** through **Ten of Wands**
Week 3. **Ace** through **Five of Cups**
Week 4. **Six** through **Ten of Cups**
Week 5. **Ace** through **Five of Swords**
Week 6. **Six** through **Ten of Swords**
Week 7. **Ace** through **Five of Pentacles**
Week 8. **Six** through **Ten of Pentacles**

Rationale for the Assignment of Attributions to the Court and Minor Cards

It is clear today that some of the most commonly accepted ideas about Tarot, especially those of late nineteenth century French and English occultists, were an arbitrary attempt to create a "secret tradition" where, as history demonstrates, none actually existed.

One who seeks a comprehensive scheme underlying the many charts and tables of attributions bequeathed by writers of that era is inevitably disappointed, or is simply frustrated by the attempt. In light of close scrutiny, a great deal of Tarot interpretation from *La Belle Epoque* is discovered to be confusing, internally inconsistent, and reflective of the writers'own personal perspective.

Thus one may legitimately seek a new plan of Court and Minor card attributions, a plan which is in agreement with the broadest aspects of the Western mystery tradition. The present scheme cannot be considered original or innovative. It is, rather, a conservative effort to relate the Tarot cards to an interpretive school at least two thousand years more ancient than the cards themselves.

In this regard, it should be emphasized that although the *Jungian Tarot* deck has been created primarily for meditation, it may be used as is any standard deck. Many people enjoy divination with the cards, a practice which has been said to promote the development of intuition and psychism. Certainly the tarot has been so linked to "fortune telling" in the past that the issue of divination must be addressed. And indeed, despite the fact that precise measurement of results is currently impossible, frequent readers of Tarot cards insist that their predictive validity is far greater than chance. If such is the case, it may be found that the *Jungian Tarot* deck, emphasizing the archetypes of the collective unconscious, produces better results than other decks.

Plan of the Minor Arcana
and of the Court Cards

Those who may find the following discussion somewhat difficult are referred to *The Qabalistic Tarot* (Robert Wang, 1983), which is available in English and in French.

The system proposed here relates card meanings to The Qabalistic Tree of Life — and to Planets in Houses — in such a way that anyone well grounded in both will know the meaning of a card in question without further study.

Through this system of attributions, serious students of astrology, many of whom may have considered the Tarot to be separate and distinct from their interests, will find a new world of symbolism in their immediate grasp. In fact, those who are already conversant with the nuances of astrology may find that they understand the Tarot better than many who have devoted years of attention to the memorization of arbitrary tables of "meanings."

Involved also is a modernization of attribution of planets to the Tree of Life.

In a revised scheme, Kether relates to Pluto; Chokmah relates to Uranus; Binah relates to Neptune; and Malkuth relates to Saturn. This allows ten specific planets with which to deal and to which values are easily assigned: One can specify a planet in a suit through a Cardinal sign, i.e., the root of Fire, Aries (Wands), the root of Water, Cancer (Cups), the root of Air, Libra (Swords), and the root of Earth, Capricorn (Pentacles). This is extremely simple:

Aces	=	Pluto
Twos	=	Uranus
Threes	=	Neptune
Fours	=	Jupiter
Fives	=	Mars
Sixes	=	Sun
Sevens	=	Venus
Eights	=	Mercury
Nines	=	Moon
Tens	=	Saturn
Wands	=	Aries
Cups	=	Cancer
Swords	=	Libra
Pentacles	=	Capricorn

So the *Ace of Wands* means Pluto in Aries. The *Ace of Cups* means Pluto in Cancer. The *Ace of Swords* means Pluto in Libra. The *Ace of Pentacles* means Pluto in Capricorn.

The plan for the Court Cards is equally direct. Personalities are defined according to the placement of Sun and Moon in a natal chart. Since all of the Wands are Aries, the *King of Wands* has the personality of a man with the Sun in Aries and the Moon in Aries. His is the personality of pure fire. The *Queen of Wands* is a personality with the Sun in Aries and the Moon in Cancer. Hers is a fiery personality tempered by Water. Generally this system tends to describe more specific human qualities, and perhaps more human frailties, then the idealized schemes of the past.

Certainly, there are a few suprises when the Minor Cards are attributed in this way. A good example is the *Five of Wands*, which has been called "Strife." But when the *Five of Wands* is related to Mars in Aries, it is seen to be a card of tremendous creative energy, of originality and of courage. It is a card of independence, of success, of popularity, and of outgoing force which may be rapidly expended.

As another example one may cite the *Three of Swords* earlier considered to be a card of pain and sorrow. But as Neptune in Libra, the positive house of Venus, it becomes a card of art, of poetry, of refinement. It is a card of love, of friendship, and of good fortune. It is the flowing Neptunian force expressed through thought (Air/Swords).

These two cards, especially, are mentioned to underscore the fact that to relate the Tarot to the mainstream of Western esoteric thought requires that we discard some deeply-ingrained notions.

The Astrological configurations on the basis of which the Court and Minor cards are explained in this book are as follows:

King of Wands: Sun in Aries and Moon in Aries
Queen of Wands: Sun in Aries and Moon in Cancer
Prince of Wands: Sun in Aries and Moon in Libra
Princess of Wands: Sun in Aries and Moon in
    Capricorn
Ace of Wands: Pluto in Aries
Two of Wands: Uranus in Aries
Three of Wands: Neptune in Aries
Four of Wands: Jupiter in Aries
Five of Wands: Mars in Aries
Six of Wands: Sun in Aries
Seven of Wands: Venus in Aries
Eight of Wands: Mercury in Aries
Nine of Wands: Moon in Aries
Ten of Wands: Saturn in Aries

King of Cups: Sun in Cancer and Moon in Aries
Queen of Cups: Sun in Cancer and Moon in Cancer
Prince of Cups: Sun in Cancer and Moon in Libra
Princess of Cups: Sun in Cancer and Moon in
    Capricorn

Ace of Cups: Pluto in Cancer
Two of Cups: Uranus in Cancer
Three of Cups: Neptune in Cancer
Four of Cups: Jupiter in Cancer
Five of Cups: Mars in Cancer
Six of Cups: Sun in Cancer
Seven of Cups: Venus in Cancer
Eight of Cups: Mercury in Cancer
Nine of Cups: Moon in Cancer
Ten of Cups: Saturn in Cancer

King of Swords: Sun in Libra and Moon in Aries
Queen of Swords: Sun in Libra and Moon in Cancer
Prince of Swords: Sun in Libra and Moon in Libra
Princess of Swords: Sun in Libra and Moon in
   Capricorn
Ace of Swords: Pluto in Libra
Two of Swords: Uranus in Libra
Three of Swords: Neptune in Libra
Four of Swords: Jupiter in Libra
Five of Swords: Mars in Libra
Six of Swords: Sun in Libra
Seven of Swords: Venus in Libra
Eight of Swords: Mercury in Libra
Nine of Swords: Moon in Libra
Ten of Swords: Saturn in Libra

King of Pentacles: Sun in Capricorn and Moon in
   Aries
Queen of Pentacles: Sun in Capricorn and Moon in
   Cancer
Prince of Pentacles: Sun in Capricorn and Moon in
   Libra
Princess of Pentacles: Sun in Capricorn and Moon in
   Capricorn

Ace of Pentacles: Pluto in Capricorn
Two of Pentacles: Uranus in Capricorn
Three of Pentacles: Neptune in Capricorn
Four of Pentacles: Jupiter in Capricorn
Five of Pentacles: Mars in Capricorn
Six of Pentacles: Sun in Capricorn
Seven of Pentacles: Venus in Capricorn
Eight of Pentacles: Mercury in Capricorn
Nine of Pentacles: Moon in Capricorn
Ten of Pentacles: Saturn in Capricorn

SUMMARY OF ATTRIBUTIONS

FOOL, Idea, Originality.
MAGICIAN, Will.
HIGH PRIESTESS, Change, Fluctuation.
EMPRESS, Fruitfulness.
EMPEROR, War.
HIEROPHANT, Ruling Power.
LOVER, Passive Inspiration.
HERMIT, Divine Inspiration.
CHARIOT, Triumph, Victory.
STRENGTH, Strength.
WHEEL OF FORTUNE, Destiny, Fate.
JUSTICE, Justice, Balance.
HANGED MAN, Enforced Suffering.
DEATH, Time, Transformation.
TEMPERANCE, Combination of Forces.
DEVIL, Material Force.
TOWER, Quarrelling, Destruction.
STAR, Hope, Faith.
MOON, Illusion, Deception.
SUN, Riches and Glory.
JUDGMENT, Final Decision.
WORLD, Basis of Action.

KING OF WANDS, Forceful, Independent.
QUEEN OF WANDS, Independent but Domestic.
PRINCE OF WANDS, Thoughtful, Observant.
PRINCESS OF WANDS, Needs Attention.
ACE OF WANDS, Birth and Death.
TWO OF WANDS, Invention.
THREE OF WANDS, Fantasy.
FOUR OF WANDS, Success.
FIVE OF WANDS, Assertiveness.
SIX OF WANDS, Impulsive Leadership.

SEVEN OF WANDS, Passion.
EIGHT OF WANDS, Rapid Flow of Ideas.
NINE OF WANDS, Volatility.
TEN OF WANDS, Control over Others.

KING OF CUPS, Intelligent, Intuitive.
QUEEN OF CUPS, Emotional, Sensitive.
PRINCE OF CUPS, Charming, Romantic.
PRINCESS OF CUPS, Practical, Ambitious.
ACE OF CUPS, Change of Feelings.
TWO OF CUPS, Adventure.
THREE OF CUPS, Secure Environment.
FOUR OF CUPS, Benevolence and Pleasure.
FIVE OF CUPS, Troubles.
SIX OF CUPS, Sympathetic Attachment.
SEVEN OF CUPS, Obstacles.
EIGHT OF CUPS, Change.
NINE OF CUPS, Vascillation.
TEN OF CUPS, Pain and Sorrow.

KING OF SWORDS, Active, Romantic.
QUEEN OF SWORDS, Socially Skillful.
PRINCE OF SWORDS, Idealistic.
PRINCESS OF SWORDS, Orderly, Seeks Power.
ACE OF SWORDS, Conflict of Ideas.
TWO OF SWORDS, Opposition and Loss.
THREE OF SWORDS, Idealism.
FOUR OF SWORDS, Imagination.
FIVE OF SWORDS, Rash Decision.
SIX OF SWORDS, Justice.
SEVEN OF SWORDS, Love.
EIGHT OF SWORDS, Intellectual Skill.
NINE OF SWORDS, Sharing.
TEN OF SWORDS, Gain through Partnership.

KING OF PENTACLES, Powerful Executive.
QUEEN OF PENTACLES, Introspective, Economical.
PRINCE OF PENTACLES, Self-assured.
PRINCESS OF PENTACLES, Steady, Ambitious.
ACE OF PENTACLES, Security Destroyed.
TWO OF PENTACLES, Reorganization.
THREE OF PENTACLES, Response to Conflict.
FOUR OF PENTACLES, Wealth.
FIVE OF PENTACLES, Responsible Authority.
SIX OF PENTACLES, Wealth through Hard Work.
SEVEN OF PENTACLES, Gain through Commerce.
EIGHT OF PENTACLES, Manipulation and Secrets.
NINE OF PENTACLES, Selfishness.
TEN OF PENTACLES, Isolated Power.
